Leadership for Learning

How to Help Teachers Succeed

Carl D. Glickman

ASCD

Association for Supervision
and Curriculum Development
Alexandria, Virginia USA

Association for Supervision and Curriculum Development
1703 N. Beauregard St. · Alexandria, VA 22311-1714 USA
Telephone: 1-800-933-2723 or 703-578-9600 · Fax: 703-575-5400
Web site: http://www.ascd.org · E-mail: member@ascd.org

ASCD publications present a variety of viewpoints. The views expressed or implied in this book should not be interpreted as official positions of the Association.

Printed in the United States of America.

January 2002 member book (pc). ASCD Premium, Comprehensive, and Regular members periodically receive ASCD books as part of their membership benefits. No. FY02-04.

ASCD Product No. 101031

ASCD member price: $19.95   nonmember price: $23.95

Library of Congress Cataloging-in-Publication Data

Glickman, Carl D.
  Leadership for learning : how to help teachers succeed / by Carl D.Glickman.
      p. cm.
Includes bibliographical references and index.
"ASCD product no. 101031"—T.p. verso.
  ISBN 0-87120-596-3 (alk. paper)
  1. School supervision—United States. 2. Teacher
effectiveness—United States. 3. Effective teaching—United States. I.
Title.
  LB2806.4 .G45 2002
  371.102—dc21   2001005294

10 09 08 07 06 05 04 03 02   10 9 8 7 6 5 4 3 2 1

Leadership for Learning

Acknowledgments

I want to thank all the school leaders—students, teachers, principals, supervisors, and superintendents across the nation—who have shared their work with me on how to make improvement of classroom teaching and learning a continuous reality. Special thanks to all the educators of the more than one hundred K–12 public schools that have been members of our Georgia League of Professional Schools and to all my associates—directors, staff, students, and faculty—of the College of Education at the University of Georgia.

I wish to note the consideration of the editors of the Jossey-Bass and Allyn and Bacon publishing companies in graciously allowing me to use passages from previous books. Readers seeking a discussion—research, concepts, and applications—of all the comprehensive domains of educational improvement in schools might refer to *Renewing America's Schools* (Jossey-Bass, 1993) and to my graduate-level textbook, *Super-Vision and Instructional Leadership: A Developmental Approach* (Allyn and Bacon, 2001), coauthored with friends Steve Gordon and Jovita Ross-Gordon.

Appreciation to ASCD and particularly to John O'Neil and Nancy Modrak for nudging me to consider writing this book as a follow-up to my 1980 ASCD book, *Developmental Supervision*, and to Anne Meek, developmental editor extraordinaire, for her immense help in making the process smooth, efficient, and joyful. The reviews of the earlier drafts of the manuscript by school leaders Mary Puryear Butler, Ray Ross, and James Pughsley were candid, exacting, and most helpful. Finally, thanks to associate Penny Nosky, who has been wonderful to work with on the development of this manuscript from locations as distant as Vermont, Crete, Bangkok, and Malaysia. Somehow, some way, Ms. Nosky was able to keep this project on task while adding value to it.

I wish to close by expressing great gratitude to my wife, Sara—wonderful teacher and eternal partner—and family members Jennifer, Volker, Rachel, Henry, Lea, Noah, Grammy Jo, Pete, Judy, and Mother Ruth for making another summer of writing, fishing, and family gatherings an always anticipated delight. There are so many others, dear friends and colleagues too numerous to mention who believe so deeply in the possibilities of education for all our students, to whom I am eternally indebted.

Preface

Writing this book has been enjoyable. I have tried to write in an easy-to-read manner what I have learned about up-close and personal work with teachers on how to improve teaching and learning in individual classrooms and schools as a whole. When ASCD first approached me about writing a book that would be derived from my book of 1980, *Developmental Supervision*, I was somewhat reluctant. More than 20 years had passed since I had written that book, and in the interval I had been centrally engaged with a network of public schools involved in whole-school change based on democratic principles for educating students. The topics of my writing had become more expansive than thinking about individual teachers and classrooms. A text I had coauthored for Allyn and Bacon, *SuperVision and Instructional Leadership*, was now in its fifth edition, and I had published two other books for Jossey-Bass on school-based renewal and the conceptual underpinnings of public education and democracy. I wondered, What could I say to teachers, principals, supervisors, and other school leaders about improving classroom teaching and learning that hadn't already been said? But then it occurred to me that, indeed, there was a better and more concise way to understand the approaches, structures, and practical applications of leadership for continuous improvement of classroom teaching and learning *within the context of whole-school improvement*.

Once I could imagine what would be fresh and practical about the treatment of these topics, I went to work. For two months then, I was at a loss to *stop* writing. My friends—in schools and districts, and in regional and national organizations—greatly helped me through several drafts of the manuscript. Soon, before I knew it, the book had written itself.

So what you are about to read is my attempt to share with my practitioner colleagues how to bring *force*, *care*, and *structure* into the process of making the often private act of classroom teaching increasingly public so that a school comes vibrantly alive with faculty and students as lifelong learners of their own practice.

1

Looking at Classroom Teaching and Learning

Look around. Listen to the noisy swarm of students become suddenly quiet as students and teachers move into classrooms and doors close. What's happening behind those doors? What are students learning? How are teachers teaching? Should you open those doors and enter, or should you stay away? How often should you visit? What should you do once you enter? How do you discover what is really going on between teacher and students? What recognition can you give to teachers who are already excelling, or what assistance can you give to those who are floundering or who are simply making it through each year? What can you do, as only one person, with responsibilities for a teaching staff of 225 or 25 or 7 in a school? As a school leader, you are bombarded with so many student needs, parent concerns, teacher concerns, and district and state requirements and paperwork that it seems futile to think of improving the teaching of every teacher. What, indeed, can you, as only one person, do?

The above scenario depicts common concerns of those who have schoolwide responsibilities for a vast array of classrooms and teachers when they contemplate frequent visits to every classroom for the pur-pose of improving learning for all students. It seems like a pipe dream for many in supervisory and instructional leadership roles, but in the most successful schools in the United States, this level of support is the day-to-day reality (Glickman, 1993; Glickman, Gordon, & Ross-Gordon, 2001). These successful schools typically have no greater amounts of time or resources than those where this scenario is a pipe dream, but the difference is how time, focus, and structure are used; how staff development, school improvement, personnel evaluation, and classroom assistance are used together; and how instructional leadership is defined and employed.

Whenever one person defines himself or herself as the sole leader, provider, and catalyst for improved classroom learning, any school with more than 15 teaching faculty immediately confronts a lack of schoolwide instructional focus and assistance. Successful schools under-stand that the direct improvement of teaching and learning in every classroom comes via a constellation of individuals and groups who undertake a myriad of activities and initiatives. These activities and ini-tiatives provide continual reflection and changing of classroom prac-tices guided by the educational aspirations of the school.

Much has happened in education in the past decade. Among the changes are new standards and assessments of learning; new account-ability schemes; new roles and responsibilities for teachers; and new forms of observations, feedback, and critique. We have much more knowledge about powerful teaching and learning. We also have sepa-rate, additional knowledge about teaching and learning for the continu-ous improvement of schools in varying geographic contexts (rural, urban, suburban) and community contexts (socioeconomic class, race, ethnicity, and gender).

So before we move into the text of explanation and application, let's dwell on the first question: Who is the person in the opening paragraph of this chapter? Who are you as a professional and as a person? Are you a student, a principal, a beginning teacher, an experienced teacher, a grade or department head, a mentor, an instructional lead teacher, an assistant principal, a central office supervisor, a curriculum or staff development director, an associate superintendent, or a superintendent? You may hold a single role or have a combination of many. For now, let's just say that your role has degrees of expectations, assumptions, status, influence, and authority that may be helpful or harmful in finding out what really is going on behind the classroom door.

Another way of asking who you are is a question of personal identity: female or male; gay or straight; Christian, Muslim, Jew, Hindu, Buddhist, agnostic, atheist, or other spiritual/religious persuasion; Southerner, Northerner, Midwesterner, Westerner, Internationalist; descendent of Europeans, Africans, Asians, Hispanics/Latinos, Native Americans, and so forth; first generation, third generation, twelfth generation; from wealth or from poverty. These personal identities are not absolutes, and they may seem irrelevant for a book on leadership for improving classroom teaching. But such identities of self and how those identities influence the perspectives of others can have a powerful impact on your efforts to open those classroom doors, possibly determining which teachers you really have access to and which understandings and priorities of learning you wish to see practiced behind the classroom doors.

Lastly, who are you as a knower, a practitioner, and a communicator of excellent classroom learning? Are you certain about what good teaching is, what it looks like in action, and how students should interact, respond, and shine? Certainty can become arrogance and dogmatism, but uncertainty can become permissiveness and the acceptance of all teaching as having equal merit. Understanding your own beliefs about good learning—whether inductive or deductive, individual or group, cooperative or competitive, paper-and-pencil-tested or performance-based, core knowledge or multicultural—is another element that can lower or raise barriers between you and what teachers do in the privacy of their own classrooms.

So think about who you are as we begin to look at ways of structuring, observing, and improving individual teaching. *Know thyself*, said Socrates. Through the ages, knowing oneself has served as a prelude to and a foundation for relating well to others.

What you read here will be useful to your immediate school world and should raise new possibilities about what *every* student deserves: teachers in every classroom who are the greatest learners of their own practice and an intellectually challenging, relevant education.

How Do Teaching and Learning Improve?

How do teaching and learning improve? Consider the boxed statement on the next page. The answer is no mystery. It's as simple as this: I cannot improve my craft in isolation from others. To improve, I must have formats, structures, and plans for reflecting on, changing, and assessing my practice.

The typical and infrequent drop-in visit by an evaluator a few times a year without continuous discussion, critiquing, and planning with others leads to the deadening and routinizing of practice and the diminishment of teaching as a profession. By definition, a *profession* is the work of persons who possess a body of knowledge, skills, and practices that must be continually tested and upgraded with colleagues. A professional field, as opposed to a technical one, is one that prizes constant dissatisfaction with one's own practice with current clients as the core to better service to clients in the future. Research has found that faculty in successful schools always question existing instructional practice and do not blame lack of student achievement on external causes. Faculty in

If, as a teacher,

- I present the same lessons in the same manner that I have used in the past;
- I seek no feedback from my students;
- I do not analyze and evaluate their work in a manner that changes my own emphasis, repertoire, and timing;
- I do not visit or observe other adults as they teach;
- I do not share the work of my students with colleagues for feedback, suggestions, and critiques;
- I do not visit other schools or attend particular workshops or seminars or read professional literature on aspects of my teaching;
- I do not welcome visitors with experience and expertise to observe and provide feedback to me on my classroom practice;
- I have no yearly individualized professional development plan focused on classroom changes to improve student learning; and finally,
- I have no systemic evaluation of my teaching tied to individual, grade/department, and schoolwide goals,

Then

I have absolutely no way to
become better as a teacher.

schools that have high intellectual standards and educate virtually all their students well work in collegial, critical ways with each other, clearly knowing what they want of all students and striving to close the gap between the rhetoric of education aims and the hard, professional work of practice. Successful schools stand in great contrast to mediocre and low-performing schools where faculty work apart from each other, without common purpose, and with self-centered beliefs that they are doing the best they can. The "source of the problem" in ordinary schools is always someone else: the students, the parents/caretakers, the school board, and so on (see Glickman, 1993, pp. 16–18).

We have now a substantial professional knowledge base on how schools succeed, how great teaching is accomplished, and how students learn well. The challenge is to use more fully what we have learned from this knowledge base. As Ron Edmonds (1979) points out in his seminal work on effective schools, "We can, whenever and wherever we choose, successfully teach all children whose schooling is of interest to us. . . . We already know more than we need to know to accomplish this task" (p. 22). Without the cultivation of dissatisfaction and critique, without being clear about our purposes, and without the need to use a knowledge base in practice, we have no education and no profession.

Organizing the Quest

To improve classroom learning for all students—preschool, elementary, middle, secondary, or postsecondary—we will use the organization of professional knowledge illustrated in Figure 1.1.

Student learning, the bull's-eye, is the focus of all that we do in classrooms and schools—the standards we set, the expectations we have, and the common mastery we expect of students in each classroom of the school. Student learning is directly influenced by the first concentric circle: the *content* or curriculum of what is taught, the teaching *methods*

1.1

Elements That Influence Student Learning in Renewing Schools and Classrooms

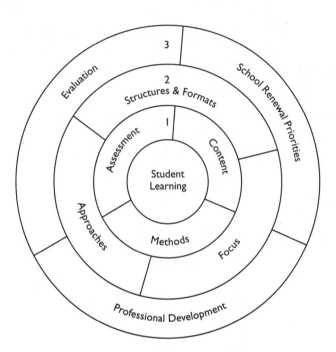

Student Learning – The focus of all we do in schools
    1. Elements That Directly Influence Students' Learning
        Content of what is taught
        Method used for teaching
        Assessment of student learning
    2. Elements That Organize Instructional Leaders' Work with Teachers
        Focus for observations and use of data
        Approaches to working with teachers
        Structures and formats for organizing instructional improvement efforts
    3. Elements That Provide the Overarching Context for Instructional Improvement
        School renewal priorities that convey the school vision
        Professional development plans and resources
        Evaluation of how and what students are learning

used, and the diagnostic *assessments* of student learning employed. Educational leaders have the tools shown in the second concentric circle to improve classroom instruction: *focus* on what to attend to in improving teaching, observing classrooms, using achievement data, and considering samples of student work; the human relation *approaches* to use to increase reflection, problem solving, and improved practice on the part of teachers; and the *structures and formats* of various ways to work individually or in groups with teachers. To have a powerful schoolwide effect, all of this work has to be embedded in the overarching third concentric circle: the overall vision and *school renewal priorities* of the school; the *professional development* plans, resources, and time provided by the school and the district; and the *evaluation* of how and what students are learning and how to use the resulting data to guide further school priorities.

   In this book, we attend to the bull's-eye of improved student learning by concentrating on circles two and three, and we conclude with how to embed this work into the entire school renewal process.

2

Structures for Classroom Assistance

"I can't do it. I don't have the time. It can't be done." If you, as a principal, assistant principal, lead teacher, department head, supervisor, or curriculum director responsible for more than 15 teachers, believe that you are the sole instructional leader, then you can't do what this book is about. However, if you understand the use of multiple structures with multiple leaders for assisting, focusing, and improving classroom teaching and learning, then continuous improvement can become an ongoing reality. These are some of the structures for classroom assistance that are most useful in schools:

- Clinical supervision
- Peer coaching
- Critical friends
- Classroom action research teams or study groups

Clinical Supervision

The best known, oldest, and most widely used structure for working directly with classroom teachers is clinical supervision (see Cogan, 1973; Costa & Garmston, 1994; Goldhammer, 1969; Pajak, 2000). It most often is used in some type of line relationship, such as supervisor to supervisee, principal to assistant principal, department head to teacher, mentor teacher to mentee, cooperating teacher to student teacher, master teacher to intern, and so on. The following explanation is derived mainly from Glickman, Gordon, & Ross-Gordon (2001, pp. 316–320).

The structure of clinical supervision can be simplified into five sequential steps.

Step 1: Pre-conference with teacher. At the *pre-conference*, the supervisor sits with the teacher and determines (1) the reason for and the purpose of the observation, (2) the focus of the observation, (3) the method and form of observation to be used, (4) the time of the observation, and (5) the time of the postconference. These determinations are made before the actual observation, so that both supervisor and teacher are clear about what will transpire. The purpose of the observation provides the criteria for the remaining decisions on focus, method, and time of observation.

Step 2: Observation of classroom instruction. The next step, observation, is the time to follow through with the understandings of the pre-conference. The observer might use any one observation or combination of observations. The observer should keep in mind the difference between *descriptions* of events and *interpretations*. Descriptions are the actual events that occurred and are recorded. Interpretations are the meanings inferred from those events.

Step 3: Analyzing and interpreting the observation and determining conference approach. The *analysis* and *interpretations* of the observation and the determination of approach are now possible. The

---

2.1

Worksheet for Analysis and Interpretations of Observation Data

Analysis: Write the major findings of your observation. Write down only what has been taken directly from your observation.

1.

2.

3.

4.

5.

Interpretations: Write below what you believe is desirable or not desirable about the major findings.

1.

2.

3.

4.

5.

---

supervisor leaves the classroom with the recorded observations and seeks solitude in an office or a corner to study the information. Regardless of the instrument, questionnaire, or open-ended form used, the supervisor makes sense out of a large mass of information. Figure 2.1 is a form that can be used to organize this task.

The last determination for the supervisor to make in Step 3 of the clinical supervision structure is to select an interpersonal approach to use with the teacher in the postconference (see Chapter 4). Should the supervisor use a directive approach by presenting observations and inter-pretations, asking for teacher input, setting a goal, and either telling the teacher what actions to take (directive-control) or providing the teacher with alternative actions to choose from (directive-informational)? Should the supervisor be collaborative by sharing the observations, allow-ing the teacher to present his or her own interpretations, and negotiating a mutual contract for future improvement? Should the supervisor be nondirective by explaining the observations and encouraging the teacher to analyze, interpret, and make his or her own plan? Some supervisors pro-vide teachers with the observation data before the postconference. This allows teachers to review the data in advance and bring their own prelim-inary interpretations to the postconference.

Step 4: Postconference with teacher. With the completed observa-tion form, the completed analysis and interpretation form, and the cho-sen interpersonal approach, the supervisor is ready to meet with the teacher in a *postconference*. The postconference is held to discuss the analysis of the observation and finally, if needed, to produce a plan for instructional improvement.

The first order of business is to let the teacher in on the recorded notes and impressions from the observation—to reflect back to the teacher what was seen. Then the supervisor can follow the chosen approach (directive-control, directive-informational, collaborative, or nondirective.) The responsibility for developing a future plan may reside with the supervisor, be equally shared, or belong to the teacher. The conference ends with a plan for further improvement. Figure 2.2 can be used to develop such a plan.

Step 5: Critique of previous four steps. The *critique* of the previous four steps is a time for reviewing whether the format and procedures from pre-conference through postconference were satisfactory and whether revisions might be needed before repeating the sequence. The

2.2

Plan for Instructional Improvement

Postconference date: _____

Time: _____

Observed teacher: _____

Clinical supervisor: _____

Objective to be worked on:

Activities to be undertaken to achieve objectives:

Resources needed:

Time and date for next pre-conference:

critique might be held at the end of the postconference or in a separate conference a few days later. It need not be a formal session but can be a brief discussion, consisting of questions such as the following: What was valuable in what we have been doing? What was of little value? What changes could be suggested? The critique has both symbolic and functional value. It indicates that the supervisor is involved in an improvement effort in the same way as the supervisee. Furthermore, the feedback from the teacher gives the supervisor a chance to decide on what practices to continue, revise, or change when working with the teacher in the future.

The five steps are now complete, and the teacher has a tangible plan of action. The supervisor is prepared to review the plan in the next pre-conference and reestablish focus and method of observation.

Peer Coaching

Peer coaching is a structure whereby fellow teachers, as each other's colleagues, conduct cycles of clinical supervision with each other with the overall coordination of a facilitator/leader (see Glickman, Gordon, & Ross-Gordon, 2001, pp. 323–326.)

The first step is a meeting with teachers to discuss how a proposed peer coaching program would fit into the instructional goals of a school or district and then to decide on the specific purposes of the program. For example, if the purpose is simply to acquaint teachers with each other's teaching strategies, less preparation is needed than if the purpose is to provide teachers with feedback on their teaching of a particular subject, set of methods, or progress toward learning standards and then to assist them to develop congruent action plans.

Before implementation of this structure, preparation of teachers includes training on (1) understanding the purpose and procedures of peer coaching, (2) conducting a pre-conference to *determine* the focus of observations, (3) conducting and analyzing an observation to distinguish between observing and interpreting classroom events, and (4) conducting two postconferences with different approaches for developing action plans—such as using a nondirective and a collaborative approach.

Preparation should include review of a standard form for writing instructional improvement plans in the postconference. The form should be simple and easy to fill out. Each peer member should understand that a completed plan is the object of the first four clinical steps and the basis for beginning the next round of coaching. See Figure 2.2 for a sample form.

Scheduling for peer coaching should take into consideration the fact that a teacher will be less enthusiastic about the project if it means increasing the amount of personal time and energy expended beyond an already full day. Teachers are more likely to participate if time for peer coaching can be scheduled during the school day. For example, having teachers place themselves together in teams that share the same planning or lunch periods allows for pre- and postconferences during the school day. Hiring a few substitutes for two days twice a year allows teachers to be relieved of class duties so that they can observe their peers. One substitute can relieve six classroom teachers for one period at a time during a six-period schedule. Principals, assistant principals, or central office supervisors occasionally substituting in classrooms so that teachers can coach each other for one class period is a practice that not only provides relief but also shows great support for coaching. Another way of freeing time for peer observations is for teachers to release each other by periodically scheduling a videotape, lecture, or some other large-group instruction so that one teacher can teach two classes. Whatever the actual schedule used to release teachers for peer coaching, the structure requires preplanning by instructional leaders and teachers to ensure that teachers can participate without great personal sacrifice.

Another issue is arranging teams of teachers. As with most issues in education, no hard and fast rules apply. Generally, teachers should be grouped with each other so that they are comfortable together but not necessarily at identical levels of experience or competence. It may be useful to put experienced teachers with new ones, superior teachers with adequate ones, or adequate teachers with struggling ones. Team members should share some degree of understanding and comfort to begin with. Hence, it is undesirable to match people who think too much alike but also undesirable to match those who think too differently. The goal is to match people who are different but still can respect and communicate easily with each other.

In a number of schools, teachers present to the facilitator or leader a confidential list of teachers they would like to work with. The facilitator/leader then matches up preferences and creates the teams. This represents a practical approach. An ideal approach would match people based on cognitive growth. For example, a teacher with great expertise in classroom management would be matched with a teacher with recent experience with student assessments. Each teacher would have greater cognitive skills in an area that would match the needs of the other. In creating teams, the choice is between an ideal way that matches people based on cognitive concerns and a practical way that matches them based on their need for security with a new program. The practical match might be best when starting the program; after peer coaching becomes a familiar ongoing activity, the facilitator could rearrange teams with the goal of greater cognitive matching.

Another important component of a peer coaching program is the close monitoring of peer progress. A peer coaching leader/facilitator should be available to peer teams as a resource person. For example, what happens when the pre-conference concludes with an agreement to observe a teacher's verbal interaction in the classroom, and the peer coach is at a loss about where to find such an observation instrument?

The training program should answer such questions, but orientation meetings cannot cover all possible needs. A leader/facilitator needs to monitor the needs of peer teams, answer questions, provide resources, and step in to help, as needed.

An elaborate monitoring system is not necessary, however. The leader/facilitator might simply check with peer coaches every few weeks. At periodic faculty meetings, he or she might ask peer coaches to write a note on their team progress. The leader/facilitator should be sure that books, films, tapes, instruments on clinical supervision, and methods/instruments for observations are catalogued and available to teachers in the professional library.

Critical Friends

Critical friends groups were developed by the Annenberg Institute for School Reform at Brown University in conjunction with school-based renewal efforts in K–12 schools throughout the nation. The structure was first derived from the Coalition of Essential Schools and then added to by other school networks such as Accelerated Schools, the Georgia League of Professional Schools, the Southern Maine Partnership, and the Annenberg Challenge Urban and Rural School Initiatives. Critical friends strategies offer ways to build a purposeful group of teachers (generally five to eight) who, with a facilitator (internal or external), look at samples of student work or instructional problems/concerns together over the course of a school year or more. For example, each teacher might bring samples of student work (as indicators of high-, average-, or low-quality work) to a pre-arranged meeting, explain the concern with the work, and then listen carefully as colleagues analyze and suggest possible improvements. Critical friends groups typically include a peer coaching component for teachers to become familiar with each other's classrooms and to follow up on particular classroom changes individual teachers have committed to accomplish. A "tuning protocol" developed by Joseph McDonald and David Allen (see Allen, 1998) is often used to keep the group meetings focused and within a specific time limit (see Figure 2.3).

A tuning protocol is a pre-established, structured agenda with time limits and specific roles for members to follow in order to organize discussions involving information, feedback, and learnings about ways to improve instruction. "Tuning" may be thought of, as in the sense of piano tuning or a tuning fork, as a way to work through a sequence of conversations thoroughly and efficiently to find ways to help put teachers' instruction into harmony and congruence with their purposes and concerns. The idea behind the protocol is that when everyone understands the structured guide to be used, the facilitator and the members will keep the conversation from straying from the instructional goal, and the conversation will provide both "warm" feedback (suggestions about what the teacher is doing well and should continue) and "cool" feedback (ideas and critiques about teacher inconsistencies and areas for change). By determining who speaks when (see, for example, Step II of Figure 2.3), the protocol ensures that only the teacher who is seeking feedback on his or her instruction and student work is allowed to speak, providing all the necessary background information and specifying questions that he or she wants the group to answer. During the time for feedback (Step VI in Figure 2.3), only group members speak; the teacher listens. This is all done to prevent entanglements, tangents, defensiveness, and confusion. Everyone in the group knows that if the group stays within the directions and timelines, the meeting will be completed in 90 minutes, and results will be accomplished. Schools that use such protocols—or adjust the model to create their own—might find initial meetings somewhat awkward (often people are used to jumping into conversations whenever they wish or straying into noninstructional

2.3

Schedule for the Tuning Protocol Developed by Joseph McDonald and David Allen

I.   Introduction   10 min.
- Facilitator briefly introduces protocol goals, guidelines, and schedule.
- Participants briefly introduce themselves.

II. Teacher presentation   20 min.
- Teacher-presenter describes the context for student work (assignment, scoring rubric, etc.)
- Teacher-presenter poses her focusing question for feedback.
- Participants are silent.

III. Clarifying questions   5 min. (max.)
- Participants ask clarifying questions.
- Facilitator judges which questions more properly belong in warm/cool feedback (e.g., questions that involve more than a very brief, factual answer).

IV. Examination of student work samples   15 min.
- Samples of student work might be original or photocopied pieces of written work and/or video clips of presentations.

V.   Pause to reflect on warm and cool feedback   2–3 min. (max.)
- Participants may take a couple of minutes to reflect silently on what they would like to contribute to the feedback session.

VI. Warm and cool feedback   5 min.
- Participants share feedback while teacher-presenter is silent.
- Facilitator may remind participants of teacher-presenter's focusing question (Step II).

VII. Reflection   15 min.
- Teacher-presenter speaks to those comments/questions he or she chooses to.
- Facilitator may intervene to focus, clarify, etc.
- Participants are silent.

VIII. Debrief   10 min.
- Facilitator leads an open discussion of the tuning experience the group has shared: What was effective? What concerns did the process raise?

Source: Blythe, T., Allen, D., & Powell, B. S. (1999). *Looking together at student work* (p. 29). New York: Teachers College Press. © 1999 by Teachers College Press. Reprinted by permission of the publisher.

areas), but after a few instances of using such a format, they find that it becomes comfortable and extremely helpful.

A number of other formats for looking at student work have been developed or described by Blythe, Allen, & Powell, 1999; McDonald, 1996; and McDonald, 2001. But the key is to use a prescribed set of group tuning protocol steps monitored by a group facilitator/gatekeeper to ensure that there is time for the teacher to explain his or her instructional issue, time for colleagues to ask questions and gather more information about the issue, and ample time for the teacher to listen carefully rather than to defend or react to suggestions from colleagues before a plan of action is made. (The Annenberg Institute *Looking's at Student Work: A Window into the Classroom* [1999] is an excellent short video that shows actual school teams using the critical friends format.)

Classroom Action Research Teams or Study Groups

The use of action research teams or study groups in a school can be tailored more specifically to the needs or issues in that school than can clinical supervision, peer coaching, or critical friends groups. Formats for such action research teams or study groups can be adapted from external formats or developed internally. In one school, as part of everyone's school-based staff development, every faculty member is expected to join and attend one study group throughout an entire school year focused on a schoolwide instructional priority applied to his or her own classroom. Faculty meetings, faculty planning days, or team planning times are set aside for each team to accomplish the following:

1. Review their common goals.

2. Establish their own research agenda to study a student learning goal (via readings, visiting classrooms in other schools, team teaching, joint curriculum planning, attending conferences or meetings, videotaping their own or other classrooms).

3. Establish their own individual classroom action plans consisting of changes in their current teaching, assessments, and activities along with the needed resources or assistance from other study group members.

4. Collect ongoing student learning data to determine the progress being made.

5. Make progress reports on individual work to the study group and the school as a whole.

Another way to create study groups tailored to a school is to have each faculty member establish his or her own individual learning goal early in the year and then form a study group with others working toward a similar learning goal. Afterward, the same type of change, action, research, and reflection processes are used.

In both cases, the study groups *must* focus on improvements to learning in *their own* classrooms and follow (or modify) a generic action research sequence, as follows:

1. Problem Identification Phase and Data Collection
   - What is (are) the student learning goal(s) of highest priority?
   - What else do we need to know about how our students are currently performing related to this goal?
   - What do we now have as baseline data on student learning that can be used for later comparisons?

2. Planning and Implementation Phase
   - What changes in our classrooms will we make?
   - What assistance will we need from each other?
   - What will be actions and completion dates for changes in our own teaching and learning?

3. Evaluation and Reflection Phase
   - After the implementation period, what data will we gather to determine progress, or the lack thereof, and to use for further action research cycles?
   - How do we improve upon the process of action research next time?

It is important to separate the problem identification phase from the planning and implementation phase. The group needs to be clear on instructional priorities and baseline data before taking actions. A common mistake many faculties make is to simply choose a priority based on feelings (the so-called cardiac approach to evaluation: "In my heart, I think we need to do better in these areas"). To be effective, each action research team needs data to support a common focus on improvements in certain areas of standards and achievements, such as writing, critical thinking skills, and so on. They then develop plans of action, including how to assist each other and what information to collect on student performance that would demonstrate concrete evidence of progress.

A brief example might be helpful. In one school, action research groups were formed according to multigrade interdisciplinary teams. The team reviewed the previous year's state assessments of science proficiency and found that a majority of students were scoring low on certain objectives. Digging deeper into the objectives made the problem obvious. The team simply was not covering the content and application of the science content being tested. The group, not wishing to abandon their interdisciplinary work, instead developed a plan for incorporating the missing objectives in thematic units of science, technology, and the environment. They observed, coached, and reviewed samples of student work during the year related to the common instructional focus. The results from the state assessments a year later found more than 90 percent of students performing at mastery levels.

Conclusion

What is important is the presence of user-friendly structures that are supported by time and resources and congruent with school goals and priorities. The structures may involve mostly one-to-one interactions (clinical supervision or peer coaching) or group interactions (action research teams or study groups) or a combination of both (critical friends). The structures for professional interactions must have a focus on what to observe and share about teaching and student learning.

Subsequent chapters provide more examples, case studies, and illustrations of the structures. For now, simply think about what structures for continuous instructional improvement are in place in your own school and what further needs and possibilities you might contemplate. We now turn to formats for observing classroom teaching and learning and student work.

3

Formats for Focusing Observation

Many aspects of classroom teaching and learning can be observed and discussed—teacher plans and behaviors, teacher-student interactions, diagnoses of student achievement, disaggregated test score data, actual samples of student performances and achievements, and teaching demonstrations (Good & Brophy, 2000). The process for determining what to look for, with the teacher, is as important as the structures and formats for communicating feedback and making plans for further improvements. What is essential is that both parties understand what the purpose of the observation is, how this purpose fits into a larger yearlong or multiyear plan for continuous individual improvement for all faculty, how the observation will be conducted, and what data will be collected at each particular phase.

Observers may use numerous ways to collect evidence about classroom teaching and student learning, ranging from descriptive note taking of classroom events, student-to-student interactions, and teacher-student interactions; time-on-task student seating charts; diagrams of space use; video- or audiotaping; and collections of student works (see

Glickman, Gordon, & Ross-Gordon, 2001, pp. 254–273; Good & Brophy, 2000; Educational Testing Service, 1999a, 1999b). What is important to reemphasize is that an observer should be able to discriminate between *description* (the actual happenings that have been recorded) and *interpretations* (the judgments made about the happenings). As a rule of thumb, it is generally best to begin any discussions with the observed teacher by sharing descriptions before making any judgments about effectiveness or the lack thereof.

We will now look at four ways to focus an observation: (1) a comprehensive framework for teaching; (2) individually tailored, open-ended questionnaires; (3) student work (student responses, understandings, and achievements); and (4) student achievement on district and state assessments. The first and second ways represent general approaches to focusing an observation. The third and fourth apply to more narrowly focused observations.

Using Frameworks for Teaching

A well-developed framework for teaching that has wide application for observations has been developed by Charlotte Danielson (1996), with accompanying materials and training for instructional leaders developed by the Educational Testing Service (1999a, 1999b). The framework was developed from research on classroom performance assessments for teacher licensure, state performance assessment systems, the standards of the National Board for Professional Teaching Standards, and ways to assess student learning according to local, state, and national learning standards. The framework incorporates various teaching styles, particular learning goals, and the context of a particular teacher with his or her class of students in a specific subject or field of learning. The framework has wide use for (1) novice teachers striving for initial licensure with the support of a mentor, (2) experienced teachers and school leaders looking for an observation instrument for peer coaching, supervision, and evaluation of classroom practice, and (3) teachers developing teaching portfolios for attaining master teacher designations and national board certification.

The framework offers what is, in effect, a comprehensive definition or classification system of the domains, components, tasks, and subtasks of the art and science of teaching. Teachers can use it to expand their own professional knowledge base for self-improvement; mentors, coaches, and supervisors can use it with teachers to help focus observations, meetings, and plans of action.

The framework comprises four domains: (1) Planning and Preparation, (2) The Classroom Environment, (3) Instruction, and (4) Professional Responsibilities. Each domain is divided into components. For example, the domain of Instruction has five components: (1) Communicating Clearly and Accurately, (2) Using Questioning and Discussion Techniques, (3) Engaging Students in Learning, (4) Providing Feedback to Students, and (5) Demonstrating Flexibility and Responsiveness.

A leader and teacher together can use the framework to determine how broadly or narrowly to focus an observation, ranging from looking at many domains to observing a single component of a single domain. It is beyond the scope of this book to detail the usages of all the domains and components. (This is best done through reference to the Danielson book itself and the accompanying Educational Testing Service manuals and training/staff development sessions listed in the References section. For an overview of the entire framework, see Appendix B-1.) For our purposes here, an examination of one component of one domain may be helpful in understanding how the entire framework can be used to focus continuous classroom improvement (see Figure 3.1).

3.1

A Framework for Teaching

Domain 3: Instruction
Component 3c: Engaging Students in Learning

Level of Performance

Element	Unsatisfactory	Basic	Proficient	Distinguished
Representation of Content	Representation of content is inappropriate and unclear or uses poor examples and analogies.	Representation of content is inconsistent in quality. Some is done skillfully, with good examples; other portions are difficult to follow.	Representation of content is appropriate and links well with students' knowledge and experience.	Representation of content is appropriate and links well with students' knowledge and experience. Students contribute to representation of content.
Activities and Assignments	Activities and assignments are inappropriate for students in terms of their age or backgrounds. Students are not engaged mentally.	Some activities and assignments are appropriate to students and engage them mentally, but others do not.	Most activities and assignments are appropriate to students. Almost all students are cognitively engaged in them.	All students are cognitively engaged in the activities and assignments in their exploration of content. Students initiate or adapt activities and projects to enhance understanding.
Grouping of Students	Instructional groups are inappropriate to the students or to the instructional goals.	Instructional groups are only partially appropriate to the students or only moderately successful in advancing the instructional goals of a lesson.	Instructional groups are productive and fully appropriate to the students or to the instruction goals of a lesson.	Instructional groups are productive and fully appropriate to the instructional goals of a lesson. Students take the initiative to influence instructional groups to advance their understanding.
Instructional Materials and Resources	Instructional materials and resources are unsuitable to the instructional goals, or students' mentally.	Instructional materials and resources are partially suitable to the instructional goals, or students' level of mental engagement is moderate.	Instructional materials and resources are suitable to the instructional goals and engage students mentally.	Instructional materials and resources are suitable to the instructional goals and engage students mentally. Students initiate the choice, adaptation, or creation of materials to enhance their own purposes.
Structure and Pacing	The lesson has no clearly defined structure, or the pacing of the lesson is too slow or rushed, or both.	The lesson has a recognizable structure, although it is not uniformly maintained throughout the lesson. Pacing of the lesson is inconsistent.	The lesson has a clearly defined structure around which the activities are organized. Pacing of the lesson is consistent.	The lesson's structure is highly coherent, allowing for the reflection and closure as appropriate. Pacing of the lesson is appropriate for all students.

Source: Danielson, C. (1996). *Enhancing professional practice: A framework for teaching* (p. 98). Alexandria, VA: Association for Supervision and Curriculum Development. © 1996 Charlotte Danielson.

Engaging Students in Learning, Component 3c, is divided into five elements: (1) representation of content, (2) activities and assignments, (3) grouping of students, (4) instructional materials and resources, and (5) structure and pacing. A leader can observe a teacher's instructional practices in each element and then categorize those practices according to four levels: unsatisfactory, basic, proficient, and distinguished. Considered together, these elements and the performance attained by the teacher explain how well students—during classroom sessions—learn important content, skills, and understandings. A teacher who has previously struggled with students being able to master essential concepts—for example, the use of algebraic equations—can be observed and helped to find where the weakness in instruction is most pronounced: in the representation of content, the activities, the grouping of students, the materials, or the structure and pacing. Further, a teacher who previously thought of teaching as mainly the transmission of correct information or knowledge may understand through this framework that for students to learn, acquire, and use knowledge, transmission of knowledge by itself—no matter how accurately the teacher conveys that knowledge—is only one-fifth of successful instruction.

The strength of this framework is that it allows leader and teacher to decide how broad or narrow the focus of observation will be. They can decide, for example, whether to use the wide lens of observing the domains of professional classroom practice or the narrow lens of a particular component.

Other frameworks that have been developed at district and state levels can be easily tailored to a school setting. One particularly valuable and user-friendly state framework is the California Standards for the Teaching Profession, a portion of which appears in Appendix B-2 (see California Commission, 1997; Santa Cruz New Teacher Project, 1998).

Using Open-Ended Questionnaires

Another way to collect observations is through open-ended questionnaires that get at specific learning goals or features of the classroom. For example, to focus on the learning goal of higher-order thinking, the following questions might guide an observer:

What Does the Teacher Do to Assist Students
to Acquire Higher-Order Thinking Skills of:

1. *Focusing:* Defining problems and setting goals?

2. *Information gathering:* Observing to obtain information and formulate questions to seek new information?

3. *Remembering:* Storing and retrieving information?

4. *Organizing:* Comparing, classifying, observing, and representing?

5. *Analyzing:* Identifying attributes and components, relationships and patterns, main ideas, and errors?

6. *Generating:* Inferring, predicting, and elaborating?

7. *Integrating:* Summarizing and restructuring?

8. *Evaluating:* Assessing the reasonableness and quality of ideas? (Glickman, Gordon, & Ross-Gordon, 2001, p. 266)

The observer and the teacher might review the questions before the classroom visit and then determine how the observer will make running notes. Perhaps the observer will write a narrative during the lesson of what teacher and students say to each other, or observe a predetermined five or six students, or interview a few students about how they analyze, integrate, and assess the ideas just discussed in class. The idea is to focus observations through agreed upon, open-ended questions with a way of recording (for example, verbatim, segments, computer-entered, etc.) that will be helpful to later discussion with the teacher.

Looking at Student Work

Observations can focus on student achievement related to classroom- or school-based standards and expectations of quality work. In these cases, student work is observed and judged through portfolios, presentations, demonstrations, or exhibits of work. Some schools require student demonstrations of learning whereby students conduct long-term projects that integrate various disciplines and apply to a setting outside the classroom. Examples might include an environmental study useful to the community, a literature and technology study that adds to the school's resource center, or a theater and arts drama that adds to the cultural life of senior citizens. (See the *Looking at Student Work* Web site at www.lasw.org, and books by Glickman, 1998; Meier, 1995; Rural Challenge, 1999; Sizer, 1992; and Wood, 1998, for more examples.) The focus of classroom instruction in these schools usually involves student achievement as measured by district or state standardized tests, but larger sets of assessments relate to what students can *do* with their learning in real, or "authentic," settings. In such classrooms, there is a need to focus ongoing observations on actual student work.

Teachers bring samples of student exams, writings, or projects and share them with the observer or each other. They explain what each of them means by high-quality work and how it can be described in rubrics understandable to students and to each other. They analyze what they expect from students and what is preventing some students from meeting the expectations. It is easy to moan about the lack of performance of students, but it is a different matter altogether to describe the elements of performance that characterize different levels of accomplishments visible to students and colleagues—that is, the standards embedded in the student performance. One of the highest forms of professional development is "to participate with other professionals in intense, intellectual discussions over the nature of content and performance standards . . . ." "How good is good enough?" and "Good enough for whom?" (Spalding, 2000, p. 762).

Let's consider some examples of focusing on student work. Nave (2000, p. 16) relates the following example from a teacher involved with a critical friends group (CFG):

> One high school science teacher was not satisfied with the quality of her students' group presentations of their projects. She videotaped a set of presentations and showed the tape at a CFG meeting, asking for suggestions for improving the students' presentations. Her CFG colleagues offered a series of suggestions for her to try with the class that was to do the project next. The teacher implemented many of her colleagues' suggestions and also videotaped those presentations. When they viewed the second videotape, the CFG members agreed that the student presentations were much better in the second class.

Another example from Nave (2000) comes from an elementary school group in which one teacher brought ungraded student writing assignments and asked her colleagues to rank the quality of the work without knowing the names and backgrounds of the students. The result was that all the highest scores were those of white middle-class students, and the lowest scores were those of second-language learners, students of color, and students from poor families. The entire group was surprised at how unequivocal the results were. They began to ask each other troubling questions about undetected bias, learning opportunities and strategies, and clarity of expectations. Each teacher went back and did a similar analysis of student work from her or his own classroom. Subsequently a whole-school commitment to action research, critical friends, and peer coaching initiatives was launched.

Blythe, Allen, & Powell (1999) suggest kinds of questions to guide the examination of student work. The questions relate to quality of student work, teaching practice, student understanding, student growth, and student intent. See Figure 3.2.

3.2

Kinds of Questions to Guide the Examination of Student Work

About the quality of student work:
- Is the work good enough?
- What is good enough?
- In what ways does this work meet or fail to meet a particular set of standards?

About teaching practice:
- What do the students' responses indicate about the effectiveness of the prompt or assignment?
- How might the assignment be improved?
- What kinds of instruction support high-quality student performances?

About the student's understanding:
- What does this work tell us about how well the student understands the topic of the assignment?
- What initial understanding do we see beginning to emerge in this work?

About the student's growth:
- How does this range of work from a single student demonstrate growth over time?
- How can I support student growth more effectively?

About the student's intent:
- What issues or questions is this student focused on?
- What aspects of the assignment intrigued this student?
- Which parts of the assignment called forth the most effort from the student?
- To what extent is the student challenging herself? In what ways?

Source: Blythe, T., Allen, D., & Powell, B. S. (1999). *Looking together at student work* (p. 10). New York: Teachers College Press. © 1999 by Teachers College Press. Reprinted by permission of the publisher.

Looking at Student Achievement According to State Standards

With the present focus on standards and classroom or school account-ability linked to state tests, many educators are expected to use sample tests to diagnose, analyze, and focus teaching on specific content, skills, or understandings that students need in order to perform well on the state tests. Whether one agrees with such approaches is not the immediate issue; in many classrooms, schools, and districts across the country, the reality is that passing such exams is required for student advancement and graduation. Further, classrooms and schools are held accountable and receive public rewards, recognitions, and sanctions based on how well students do in absolute terms of mastery and in comparisons with other classrooms, schools, and districts.

A focus on how students have performed or scored on past tests, how to diagnose their curriculum performance, and how to plan changes in the duration, content, and methods of classroom instruction—all can become targets for classroom improvement. As an example, let's look at a high school where weighted scores for reading, language, math, sci-ence, and social studies needed to be significantly improved to increase the passing rate of students, and where diagnosis of previous test scores indicated major weaknesses in reading in the content areas, particularly reading comprehension and science, in which only 65 percent of stu-dents had performed at adequate levels. The focus for improvement for each classroom teacher became reading comprehension across the disci-plines; the focus for science teachers was additional laboratory class-room work and more frequent science tutorials and assessments. The focus for observations, feedback, and peer study groups with teachers throughout the year included looking at previous assessments and typi-cal teaching strategies and reviewing the results of recent science tests with attention to particular students who were still not making adequate progress. The outcome of the effort was considerable improvement in all targeted areas (see Allen, Rogers, Hensley, Glanton, & Livingston, 1999; Calhoun, 1994; Schmoker, 1999; and Weis, 2000 for additional examples).

A different example of using state results is the actual case of Monarch Elementary School, with five grades and 800 students, more than half of whom were from low socioeconomic backgrounds. The school had done extraordinarily well in terms of student pass rates on statewide tests: 98 percent in reading, 100 percent in writing, and 97 percent in mathematics. Monarch's results, thus, were far above the state average. But even so, the faculty was not content. Rallis and MacMullen (2000) describe the faculty meeting at which the results were presented and what occurred afterward in the school:

> Marty (4th grade teacher): It's good to hear that our kids did so well. But I'm still a bit skeptical. I just don't feel that all my students know the material that well. Maybe we ought to look a bit more closely at the score reports. I still have some questions.
>
> Yvonne (4th grade teacher): I think we need to ask exactly what 98 percent passing means. What does "passing" mean?
>
> As the members of the group examine the reports from the state testing bureau, they notice gaps between the high percentage of students who passed and the lower percentage of those who mastered all the objectives. For example, Marty sees that while 96 percent of the fourth graders passed in reading comprehension, only 62 percent mastered all the objectives. Yvonne notes that the gap is even larger—96 percent passing versus 40 percent mastery—in math. They discover that the standard for passing actually means meeting minimum expectations.
>
> In response to this discovery, they decide to focus their inquiry on the gap between passing and mastery. Soon, they are generating questions about student learning. What does it mean to meet minimum

expectations? What does it mean to master an objective? Which objectives do students master? Which are they not mastering? Which students master them and which do not? Does mastery tend to clump along lines of gender, race, socioeconomic status?

These questions on learning generate questions about teaching. What are we actually doing in our classrooms? What programs do we use, and are we following them? Do our standards and objectives match those of the tests? If not, how do we reconcile the test with our curriculum? Are we teaching for mastery or for minimum expectations? How are students responding to each program? (p. 767)

The Monarch School Council then decides to respond to these questions as the focus for critical friends groups and peer coaching for the upcoming school year.

Why Such a Stress on Clarifying the Focus for Observation?

Individuals involved in observations should discuss and act upon only what they agreed to focus on. It certainly is appropriate to do a few general observations to gain an overall feel for a classroom and for a teacher to become comfortable with another adult in his or her setting. But after a point, if the leader and the teacher don't know what is being looked at together, then discussions predictably will move away from issues of teaching and learning to issues outside the classroom (such as individual misbehavior of students, parent needs, school politics, personal issues, and so on). It is not that the latter issues are unimportant. People do need time to talk about noninstructional issues. But study after study shows that teachers and leaders rarely talk about the professional reason for being in teaching: improving learning for all students (see DiPardo, 1999). The cultural norms and routines of most schools simply reflect an unspoken expectation that teachers will be instructionally private and isolated from each other, without collegial support or a frame for talking openly about teaching and learning. To talk deeply, wisely, and practically about teaching and learning means that *leadership*, *force*, *structure*, and *focus* must permeate the entire school environment. In the next chapter, we will examine various interpersonal approaches and applications to working with individuals.

4

Approaches to Working Closely with Teachers

S
hirley Horvback is an English teacher in her 12th year at New Castle High School. She is married, has no children, and lives in a high-socioeconomic neighborhood 20 miles from the low-socioeconomic neighborhood of her school. A major reason that Ms. Horvback teaches at New Castle is her desire "to help students from such impoverished surroundings acquire an appreciation for literature." She is an avid reader of both contemporary and classic literature and occasionally writes her own short stories.

Ms. Horvback generally is regarded as a competent teacher. She has a rather bombastic manner of speaking and with her large, robust, and rangy physical stature creates an imposing presence. Many of her students are afraid of her, and the word is passed quickly around to new students that "you don't mess with Ol' Lady Horvback." Most students grudgingly believe that her classes are worthwhile. When the hard work and teacher pressure are over, students seem to emerge from her class as better readers and writers.

Ms. Horvback, except for one close friend, is not liked by the other teachers at New Castle. They complain of her arrogant, elitist attitude. She conveys the *impression that New Castle High is privileged to have such a literate person as herself on its staff. She lets it be known that she was once accepted as a Ph.D. student in English at a prestigious university but turned down the opportunity so she could teach at New Castle. At faculty meetings, Ms. Horvback's sense of superiority is evident. She has an answer to every problem; she is insightful; she analyzes and proposes thorough solutions; and she can easily suggest what others should do to make New Castle a better school. But when it comes to action, she backs off. Ms. Horvback is usually the last teacher to arrive at school in the morning, the first to leave in the afternoon.*

If you were working with Ms. Horvback, what else would you like to know about her? What else do you need to know about yourself in relation to her? What kind of "up-close" work can help Ms. Horvback improve her classroom instruction, and also the learning climate of the school?

On the other hand, consider the following, very different, scenario.

Frank Apanka is a young Caribbean American, raised in poverty in the urban Midwest, a cum laude graduate from a city college. After four years as an associate at a major investment firm, he decided to take a major cut in pay and pursue a teaching career in a rural elementary school with an increasing second-language and migrant population of students. He is a specialist in upper-level mathematics and science. He has vim, vigor, and passion but has run up against students he literally can't understand, a set of high-stakes state standards and tests that he finds overwhelming and intrusive, and a faculty that is predominantly mature, experienced, white, and middle class.

Mr. Apanka is one of the lateral-entry teachers—degreed individuals who are noneducation majors entering the teaching profession. He cares quite deeply about students and believes in the importance of science and mathematics in their later lives. Although he is still completing the requirements for provisional certification, he constantly volunteers for extra duties, such as to head the student science fair, to serve on the school climate committee, and to staff the tutorial program three mornings a week before school. Other faculty see him as a joiner, a leader, and an idealist who always verges on the edge of being overcommitted.

How do you—as principal, supervisor, colleague, or mentor—work with Mr. Apanka? What else do you need to know about him, his classroom, his subject, his concerns, and his relations with students, parents, faculty, and others? How might you approach and work with him?

Instructional Leadership Approaches and Behaviors

In an earlier work, I defined four basic approaches to working with teachers on classroom issues based on the clustering of types of verbal and non-verbal behaviors (Glickman, 1980). We will draw on that work in considering the behaviors that might be used in conference with Ms. Horvback, Mr. Apanka, or others. These behaviors—listening, clarifying, encouraging, reflecting, presenting, problem solving, negotiating, directing, standardizing, and reinforcing—appear in Figure 4.1. We will begin to see how these behaviors relate to certain clusters or approaches. But first, here are explanations of each category:

• **Listening.** The instructional leader sits quietly and looks at the speaker and nods his or her head to show understanding. Nodding and guttural utterances ("uh-huh," "ummm," and so on) also indicate listening.

• **Clarifying.** The instructional leader asks questions and statements to clarify the speaker's point of view: "Do you mean that?" "Would you explain this further?" "I'm confused about this," "I lost you on . . . ," "You lost me . . . ."

• **Encouraging.** The instructional leader provides acknowledgment responses that help the speaker continue to explain his or her

4.1

The Instructional Leader Behavior Continuum

	1	2	3	4	5	6	7	8	9	10	
T	**Listening**	**Clarifying**	**Encouraging**	**Reflecting**	**Presenting**	**Problem solving**	**Negotiating**	**Directing**	**Standard-izing**	**Reinforcing**	**t**
t											**L**

Categories of behaviors:	Nondirective	Collaborative	Directive-Informational	Directive-Control

Key

T = maximum teacher responsibility   L = maximum instructional leader responsibility

t = minimum teacher responsibility   l = minimum instructional leader responsibility

Source: Adapted from Glickman, C. D. (1980). Developmental supervision: Alternative practices for helping teachers to improve instruction. Alexandria, VA: Association for Supervision and Curriculum Development; Glickman, C. D., Gordon, S. P., & Ross-Gordon, J. V. (2001). Supervision and instructional leadership: A developmental approach (5th ed.). Boston: Allyn and Bacon. Reprinted by permission of the publisher.

positions: "Yes, I'm following you," "Continue on," "Ah, I see what you're saying—tell me more."

- **Reflecting.** The instructional leader summarizes and paraphrases the speaker's message for verification of accuracy: "I understand that you mean . . . ," "So, the issue is . . . ," "I hear you saying . . . ."

- **Presenting.** The instructional leader gives his or her own ideas about the issue being discussed: "This is how I see it . . . ," "What can be done is . . . ," "I'd like us to consider . . . ," "I believe that . . . ."

- **Problem Solving.** The instructional leader takes the initiative, usually after a preliminary discussion of the issue or problem, in pressing all those involved to generate a list of possible solutions. This is usually done through statements such as "Let's stop and each write down what can be done," "What ideas do we have to solve this problem?" "Let's think of all possible actions we can take."

- **Negotiating.** The instructional leader moves the discussion from *possible* to *probable* solutions by discussing the consequences of each proposed action, exploring conflict or priorities, and narrowing down choices with questions such as these: "Where do we agree?" "How can we change that action to be acceptable to all?" "Can we find a compromise that will give each of us part of what we want?"

- **Directing.** The instructional leader tells the participant(s) either what the choices are or what is to be done. To explain the choices, the leader can say such things as this: "As I see it, these are the alternatives: You could do A, B, or C. Which of these makes the most sense to you and which will you use?" If the leader tells the participants what is to be done, he or she may say: "I've decided that we will do . . . ," "I want you to do . . . ," "The policy will be . . . ," "This is how it is going to be . . . ," "We will then proceed as follows."

- **Standardizing.** The instructional leader sets the expected criteria and the timeline or time frame for the decision to be implemented.

Target objectives are set. Expectations are conveyed with statements such as these: "By next Monday, we want to see . . . ," "Report back to me on this change by . . . ," "Have the first two activities carried out by . . . ," "I want an improvement of 25 percent involvement by the next meeting," "We have agreed that all tasks will be done before the next observation."

- **Reinforcing.** The instructional leader strengthens the directive and the criteria to be met by telling of possible consequences. Possible consequences can be positive, in the form of praise: "I know you can do it!" "I have confidence in your ability!" "I want to show others what you've done!" Consequences also can be negative: "If it's not done on time, we'll lose the support of . . . ," or "It must be understood that failure to get this done on time will result in . . . ."

These behaviors of conferencing can be put together in different combinations that form different approaches and outcomes for working with teachers. Some behaviors place more responsibility on the teacher(s) to make the decision, others place more responsibility on the instructional leader to make the decision, and still others indicate a shared responsibility for decision making. The categories of behaviors are listed in a sequence on the instructional leader behavior continuum shown in Figure 4.1 to reflect the scale of control or power.

When an instructional leader *listens* to the teacher, *clarifies* what the teacher says, *encourages* the teacher to speak more about the concern, and *reflects* by verifying the teacher's perceptions, then clearly the teacher participates in making the decisions about professional practice. The instructional leader's role is that of an active prober or a sounding board for the teacher to make his or her own decisions. The teacher has high control, and the leader low control, over the actual decision (big *T* for teacher, small *l* for leader). This is seen as a *nondirective interpersonal approach.*

When a leader uses nondirective behaviors to understand the teacher's point of view but then participates in the discussion by *presenting* his or her own ideas, *problem solving* by asking all parties to propose possible actions, and then *negotiating* to find a common course of action satisfactory to teacher and leader, then the control over the decision is shared by all. This is viewed as a *collaborative interpersonal approach*.

When an instructional leader *directs* the teacher on the alternatives the teacher may choose from, and, after the teacher selects, the leader *standardizes* the timeline and criteria of expected results, then the leader is the major source of information, providing the teacher with restricted choice (small *t*, big *L*). This is viewed as a *directive-informational interpersonal approach*.

Finally, when a leader *directs* the teacher in what will be done, *standardizes* the timeline of and criteria for expected results, and *reinforces* the consequences of action or inaction, then the leader has taken responsibility for the decision (small *t*, big *L*). The leader is clearly determining the actions for the teacher to follow. These behaviors are called a *directive-control interpersonal approach*.

Outcomes of the Conference

Another way to clarify the distinctions among approaches is to look at the outcomes of the conference and determine who controls the final decision for instructional improvement. Using the nondirective approach, the leader facilitates the teacher's thinking in developing a self-plan. In the collaborative approach, both leader and teacher share information and possible practices as equals in arriving at a mutual plan. In the directive-informational approach, the leader provides the focus and the parameters of possible actions, and the teacher is asked to choose from among the leader's suggestions. In the directive-control approach, the leader tells the teacher what to do. Nondirective provides maximum teacher choice; collaborative, mutual choice; directive-informational, selected choice; and directive-control, no choice in the outcome of the conference. See Figure 4.2.

Clarifying Your Own Approach

In determining the approach to use, the leader should take into account the commitment, expertise, and needs of individual teachers. The goal is always to use approaches that strengthen a teacher's capacity for greater reflection and self-reliance in making improvements in classroom teaching and learning. However, all leaders should first understand themselves, their predominant ways of interacting, and their core beliefs about working with others. Every leader—like every human being—has a preferred style for communicating with others, whether it be assertive and bold, calm and conversational, or quiet and reassuring. This does not mean that leaders are static and fixed in their interpersonal approaches, but when they digress to a different approach, others may note that they are "acting out of character." So it is with ways leaders work with teachers.

What is your predominant approach: nondirective, collaborative, directive-informational, or directive-control? How do you know what it is? Often people think of themselves differently than do those who work

4.2

Interpersonal Approaches, Outcomes, and Levels of Choice

Approach	Outcome	Choice
Nondirective	Teacher self-plan	Maximum teacher choice
Collaborative	Mutual plan	Mutual choice
Directive-informational	Leader-suggested plan	Selected choice
Directive-control	Leader-assigned plan	No teacher choice

with them. I have known a few autocratic, directive-control leaders who sincerely believe that they are purely collaborative. When they state this belief, those who know them well roll their eyes. These leaders are not being knowingly deceptive; they really do think they exhibit one approach while practicing another.

You can use either of two simple methods to help you clarify your understanding of your approach to working with teachers on classroom issues. The first method is to ask those you work with to simply identify which of the four overall approaches you most often use with them in matters of individual classroom assistance. The second method is to fill out the Instructional Leadership Beliefs Inventory (Figures 4.3 and 4.4) on yourself, *and*, at the same time, ask those you work with to anonymously fill out the survey as well, to reveal how they see you in action. The survey has no great scientific validity but is simply a way to open up awareness of your own practices.

The inventory is designed for leaders—referred to as supervisors in the inventory—to assess their own beliefs. It assumes that leaders believe and act according to all four of the orientations, yet one usually dominates. The inventory is designed to be self-administered and self-scored. The second part lists items for which leaders must choose one of two options. A scoring key follows, which can be used to compare the predictions of Part I with the actual beliefs indicated by the forced-choice items of Part II.

What to Do with the Approaches?

A leader with a rudimentary understanding of these four approaches to working with individual teachers—nondirective, collaborative, directive-informational, and directive-control—can now put this understanding into practice. The idea is that a leader needs to understand the teacher (his or her needs, experiences, identity, and development), the instructional focus under

4.3

Instructional Leadership Beliefs
Inventory Part I: Predictions

Check one answer for each question.

Questions	About 100% of the time	About 75% of the time	About 50% of the time	About 25% of the time	About 0% of the time
How often do you use a *directive-informational* or *-control approach* (rather than either of the other two approaches)?	———	———	———	———	———
How often do you use a *collaborative approach* (rather than either of the other two approaches) in supervising teachers?	———	———	———	———	———
How often do you use a *nondirective approach* (rather than the other two approaches) in supervising teachers?	———	———	———	———	———

Author's note: This is a slight modification of an instrument originally developed by Dr. Roy T. Tamashiro and me.

4.4

Instructional Leadership Beliefs Inventory
Part II: Forced Choices

Circle either A or B for each item. You may not completely agree with either choice, but choose the one that is *closest to how you feel.*

1. A. Leaders should give teachers a large degree of autonomy and initiative within broadly defined limits.

    B. Leaders should give teachers directions about methods that will help them improve their teaching.

2. A. It is important for teachers to set their own goals and objectives for professional growth.

    B. It is important for leaders to help teachers reconcile their personalities and teaching styles with the philosophy and direction of the school.

3. A. Teachers are likely to feel uncomfortable and anxious if the objectives on which they will be evaluated are not clearly defined by the leader.

    B. Evaluations of teachers are meaningless if teachers are not able to define with their leaders the objectives for evaluation.

4. A. An open, trusting, warm, and personal relationship with teachers is the most important ingredient in supervising teachers.

    B. A leader who is too informal and friendly with teachers risks being less effective and less respected than a leader who keeps a certain degree of professional distance from teachers.

5. A. My role during conferences is to make the interaction positive, to share realistic information, and to help teachers plan their own solutions to problems.

    B. The methods and strategies I use with teachers in a conference are aimed at our reaching agreement over the needs for future improvement.

(continued)

4.4 (continued)

Instructional Leadership Beliefs Inventory
Part II: Forced Choices

6. *In the initial phase of working with a teacher ...*
   A. I develop objectives with each teacher that will help accomplish school goals.
   B. I try to identify the talents and goals of individual teachers so they can work on their own improvement.

7. *When several teachers have a similar classroom problem, I prefer to ...*
   A. Have the teachers form an ad hoc group and help them work together to solve the problem.
   B. Help teachers on an individual basis find their strengths, abilities, and resources so that each one finds his or her own solution to the problem.

8. *The most important clue that an inservice workshop is needed is when ...*
   A. The leader perceives that several teachers lack knowledge or skill in a specific area that is resulting in low morale, undue stress, and less effective teaching.
   B. Several teachers perceive the need to strengthen their abilities in the same instructional area.

9. A. The formal leadership staff should decide the objectives of an inservice workshop because they have a broad perspective of the teachers' abilities and the school's needs.
   B. Teachers and the formal leadership staff should reach consensus about the objectives of an inservice workshop before the workshop is held.

10. A. Teachers who feel they are growing personally will be more effective in the classroom than teachers who are not experiencing personal growth.
    B. The knowledge and ability of teaching strategies and methods that have been proven over the years should be taught and practiced by all teachers to be effective in their classrooms.

4.4

....

Instructional Leadership Beliefs Inventory
Part II: Forced Choices

11. *When I perceive that a teacher might be scolding a student unnecessarily . . .*

    A. I explain, during a conference with the teacher, why the scolding was excessive.

    B. I ask the teacher about the incident but do not interject my judgments.

12. A. One effective way to improve teacher performance is to formulate clear behavioral objectives and create meaningful incentives for achieving them.

    B. Behavioral objectives are rewarding and helpful to some teachers but stifling to others; also, some teachers benefit from behavioral objectives in some situations but not in others.

13. *During a pre-observation conference . . .*

    A. I suggest to the teacher what I could observe, but I let the teacher make the final decision about the objectives and methods of observation.

    B. The teacher and I mutually decide the objectives and methods of observation.

14. A. Improvement occurs very slowly if teachers are left on their own; but when a group of teachers works together on a specific problem, they learn rapidly and their morale remains high.

    B. Group activities may be enjoyable, but I find that individual, open discussion with a teacher about a problem and its possible solutions leads to more sustained results.

15. *When an inservice or staff development workshop is scheduled . . .*

    A. All teachers who participated in the decision to hold the workshop should be expected to attend it.

    B. Teachers, regardless of their role in forming a workshop, should be able to decide if the workshop is relevant to their personal or professional growth and, if not, should not be expected to attend.

(continued)

4.4 (continued)

Instructional Leadership Beliefs Inventory
Part II: Forced Choices

Scoring Key

Step 1. Circle your answer from Part II of the inventory in the columns below:

Column I	Column II	Column III
1B	1A	
	2B	2A
3A	3B	
4B		4A
	5B	5A
6A		6B
	7A	7B
8A		8B
9A	9B	
10B		10A
11A		11B
12A	12B	
	13B	13A
14B	14A	
	15A	15B

Step 2. Tally the number of circled items in each column and multiply by 6.7.

2.1.   Total responses in Column I   _____   X 6.7 = _____

2.2.   Total responses in Column II   _____   X 6.7 = _____

2.3   Total responses in Column III   _____   X 6.7 = _____

(continued)

4.4

Instructional Leadership Beliefs Inventory
Part II: Forced Choices

Step 3. Interpretation

The product you obtained in Step 2.1 is an approximate percentage of how often you take a *directive approach* (informational or control) with teachers, rather than either of the other two approaches. The product you obtained in Step 2.2 is an approximate percentage of how often you take a *collaborative approach*, and Step 2.3 is an approximate percentage of how often you take a *nondirective approach*. The approach on which you spend the greatest percentage of time is the leadership model that dominates your beliefs. If the percentage values are equal or nearly equal, you take an eclectic approach.

You can also compare these results with your predictions in Part I.

consideration and the related student learning, and the context of the classroom in determining which approach might both meet the immediate learning need and facilitate over time the teacher's own progress toward reflective, more autonomous, action research. Again, keep in mind that an instructional leader can be a principal or an assistant principal, a central office supervisor, a master teacher, a mentor teacher, a peer coach, or some other role with a responsibility to facilitate the improvement of classroom teaching and learning of a spupervisee, a colleague, or a new teacher.

Now that you have a clearer understanding of how you most often interact with faculty and are aware of behaviors and approaches for working with individual teachers, how might you assist Ms. Horvback and Mr. Aanka? Should you treat them alike or differently? Where might you begin? What knowledge about each as individuals and professionals should you consider?

5

Direct Applications to Assisting Teachers

I n this chapter, case studies and narrative scripts delineate the four approaches to working with teachers. Each approach is presented within the clinical supervision structure for consistency, but the approaches also apply within the other structures of peer coaching, critical friends, and action research teams. The approaches are equally appropriate for working with individuals or groups. The scripts show leaders' efforts with teachers of various grade levels and subjects and include additional ways of observing and planning not mentioned in previous chapters.

A warning: You may find the narrations of all these cases to be too detailed and technical (i.e., boring!), detracting you from the flow of the book. Thus, my advice is to read at least one case and approach for a sense of the interplay between leadership and teacher behaviors and then either continue to other narrations or skip to Chapter 6. That chapter provides assistance in making judgments for when and how to use particular approaches according to stage of development, interpersonal identity, and competence levels of teachers.

To clarify the use of the various approaches, we will examine the work of different instructional leaders with Bob Finer, a middle school science teacher; Susan Valdock, a 4th grade teacher; and Herbert Klunger, a high school English teacher. The clinical format will be the same so that the reader can focus on the applications of the particular approaches—directive-control, directive-informational, collaborative, and nondirective.

The Directive-Control Approach: An Example

A directive-control orientation includes the major behaviors of clarifying, presenting, demonstrating, directing, standardizing, and reinforcing. The final outcome is an assignment for the teacher to carry out over a specified period of time.

> Bob Finer, a middle school science teacher, is encountering a great deal of trouble with three students in his class. These students are constantly talking out of turn, starting fights, and poking other classmates. Mr. Finer finds their behavior disturbing and sees that other normally well-behaved students are beginning to misbehave. Science class is rapidly deteriorating into wasted time.

The leader has made a few random visits to Mr. Finer's classroom to deliver messages and materials. Based on those observations and on often hearing Mr. Finer's angry voice and seeing a steady procession of students sent to the school office, the leader has determined that Mr. Finer is experiencing discipline and management problems. With this in mind, she arranges a meeting with the teacher.

The leader has analyzed what the teacher needs and is proceeding on the basis that Mr. Finer needs definite, immediate, and concrete help to get the class "turned around." Time is being wasted, and Mr. Finer needs to be told what to do. Standards of performance need to be determined, and a timeline of specific teacher actions must be assigned. A directive leader might engage Mr. Finer in the following manner.

Pre-conference

The leader is seated behind her desk as Mr. Finer walks in. She asks him to be seated in a chair directly across from her. The leader begins by presenting her thoughts.

Leader: "Bob, I detect that you are having problems with some of your students in 5th period class. I would like to help you in making that class more attentive."

Mr. Finer (shrugging): "It's not too bad. I'll get them under control."

Leader: "I'm sure you will, but time is moving on, and I'd like to help. I'm planning to visit the class tomorrow for the entire period."

Mr. Finer (again shrugs his shoulders): "Well, I'm showing a film tomorrow, so I don't know how much you'll get to see."

Leader: "All right, I'll be in the next day. Listen, I'm going to closely observe the students during the class and see how attentive they are. Perhaps I can get some clues as to why they lose attention."

Mr. Finer: "I can give you a clue. Watch James, Matthew, and Regina. Watch how they get everyone going."

Leader: "Fine. I'll use an instrument to record the behavior of those three students. If they are the source of the problem, we can come up with a plan for keeping them under control. See you in two days."

The leader has clearly been in charge of this pre-conference. She has classified the problem, checked it out with the teacher, and outlined how she will observe the class. She has listened to the teacher to verify or revise her own thinking, but she has not encouraged the teacher to talk on. The leader wants immediate, direct action and deflects any teacher hesitancies. The leader is not hostile or intimidating; instead, she is businesslike, serious, and task oriented.

Classroom Observation

During the observation, the leader uses a checklist at five-minute intervals (see Figure 5.1). Each time she observes one of the students listening to the teacher, engaging in classroom discussion, or doing assigned work, she puts a check in the "Attentive to Task" box. When she sees one of the students vacantly staring into space or sitting with his or her head on the desk, she puts a check in the "Inattentive/Passive" box. Each time one of

5.1
Checklist for an Observation of Student Behavior

	Attentive to Task	Inattentive/Passive	Inattentive/Active
1:10			
1:15			
1:20			
1:25			
1:30			
1:35			
1:40			
1:45			
1:50			
1:55			

the three students is out of his or her seat, wandering around, talking with others about nonschool matters, fighting, or displaying other disruptive behavior, the leader puts a check in the "Inattentive/Active" box. Each student is given an initial observation and nine additional five-minute observations during the class period. At the end of the class, the leader asks Mr. Finer to meet with her to discuss the observation.

Analysis and Interpretation

Back in her office, the leader reviews the completed form (see Figure 5.2) and prepares for the postconference. She quickly concludes that the three students were attentive for only 6 observations out of 30, or 20 percent of the time. On further analysis, she notices that the students began as attentive, moved to passive inattention, and then to active

5.2			
Completed Checklist for an Observation of Student Behavior			
	Attentive to Task	Inattentive/Passive	Inattentive/Active
1:10	XXX		
1:15	XX	X	
1:20		XXX	
1:25		XX	X
1:30			XXX (entire class noisy)
1:35		XXX	
1:40		XX	X
1:45	X	X	X
1:50		X	XX
1:55		XXX	

inattention. After that point the best that Mr. Finer could do was to yell at them to get passive inattention. Only once did a student get back to "Attentive to Task." The leader concludes that Mr. Finer must not only stop their disruptive behavior (Inattentive/Active) but must also get them back to the task more frequently. If not, the leader concludes, Mr. Finer is fighting a losing battle with the three students. The leader concurs with Mr. Finer's previous judgment that the three students do appear to instigate trouble with the rest of the students. The leader sits back to consider thoughtfully what she will tell Mr. Finer.

Postconference

The following dialogue takes place after the leader has reviewed the completed observation instrument with the teacher.

Leader: "So, Bob, you can see that you're fighting a holding action. When you get James, Matthew, and Regina to stop their misbehavior, you have to get them actively engaged in learning, or else they are soon clowning around again."

Mr. Finer: "Well, yeah, but when I tell them to do something, they don't."

Leader: "That may be true, but when I was observing, you were telling them to stop and not telling them what to do."

Mr. Finer: "But they don't want to do their work."

Leader: "Then I think you need a threefold attack. First, get them away from each other. Second, give them each an individual project they will enjoy doing. Use it as a reward for finishing their assigned work. Third, remind them of what they are to do, not what *not* to do. At times, you might even move over to one of them, pick up his hand with the pencil, open the book to the correct page, and show him what should be done."

Mr. Finer: "Well, okay, but I'm not sure I can find a special project for them."

Leader: "Tomorrow I'll take over your class. For the first half hour, observe how I correct them and see if it works. For the second half of the period, visit Mrs. Kitchen's class and see what kinds of individual science projects she has."

Mr. Finer: "Okay, I'll do what you say, but I'm still not sure if it will work."

Leader: "We don't know unless we try; you can do it. So here's your assignment. Tomorrow you are to, first, observe me teaching a demonstration lesson and, second, observe Mrs. Kitchen's science class and the various projects. Then for the next two weeks you are to try three techniques. Start by giving James, Matthew, and Regina a special project to do when they finish their work. Then, when you correct them, tell them what to do, even show them. Last, change their seating pattern so they are more than two seats away from each other. Put some distance between them.

I'll be back in your classroom two weeks from today, same period, and I want to see if you have increased their attentive time to at least 50 percent. Any questions?"

Mr. Finer: "No, I don't think so. What if I don't get 50 percent of attentive time?"

Leader: "I think that you can. Let me see if I can get you those extra dissection kits that you've been wanting."

Postanalysis

The following morning, the leader and the teacher converse in the hall.

Leader: "What do you think about what we've done up to now?"

Mr. Finer: "I'm still not sure if all this will help, but at least I have directions to follow. I was really floundering before."

Leader: "If it doesn't work, I have some other ideas to try later on. But I think it will."

Discussion: The Directive-Control Approach

The directive leader "took the bull by the horns"; and after thinking carefully about Bob Finer's situation, she collected data, presented it, and gave the teacher a two-week action assignment. She carefully detailed what the teacher was to do and what the criteria for improvement were. The leader engaged primarily in the behaviors of *clarifying* and *presenting* her thinking, *directing* what should happen, *demonstrating* appropriate teaching behaviors, and *standardizing* a target level of student progress. The leader used praise and rewards as an incentive and as a *reinforcement* for carrying out the plan. (In such a situation, attempting to please the leader might be sufficient incentive by itself.)

The directive-control approach should not be confused with arbitrary, capricious, or totalitarian behavior. The directive leader has judged that the most effective way to improve instruction is by making standards clear and by tangibly showing teachers how to attain such standards. It is a thoughtful, businesslike, and unilateral approach based on a careful collection of data. The approach presumes that the leader knows more about the context of teaching and learning than the teacher does or has superior analytical skills and problem-solving abilities. Therefore, the leader's decisions are likely to be more effective than if the teacher is left to his or her own devices.

As we see in Figure 5.3, the leader employs directive behaviors to develop a detailed assignment for the teacher. Although the sequence may vary, the leader's dominant behaviors are the following:

5.3

Instructional Leader Behavior Continuum: Directive Approach

	1	2	3	4	5	6	7	8	9	10	
T	Listening	Clarifying	Encouraging	Presenting	Problem Solving	Negotiating	Demonstrating	Directing	Standardizing	Reinforcing	t
											L
		(a) Leader clarifies teacher's problems.		(b) Leader presents ideas on what and how information will be collected.			(d) Leader demonstrates appropriate teaching behavior.	(c) Leader directs teacher on what actions will take place.	(e) Leader sets baseline data and standard for improvement.	(f) Leader uses material or social incentives.	

Product: Assignment for the teacher

Key:

T = Maximum teacher responsibility   L = Maximum leader responsibility
t = Minimum teacher responsibility   l = Minimum leader responsibility

● **Clarifying**—The leader clarifies the teacher's problem and perhaps asks the teacher for confirmation or revision.

● **Presenting**—The leader presents his or her own ideas on what information should be collected and how it will be collected.

● **Directing**—The leader directs the teacher, after data collection and analysis, on the actions that need to be taken.

● **Demonstrating**—The leader demonstrates for the teacher appropriate teaching behavior or asks the teacher to observe in another classroom.

● **Standardizing**—The leader sets the standard for improvement based on the preliminary baseline information.

● **Reinforcing**—The leader reinforces teacher behavior by using material or social incentives.

The Directive-Informational Approach: An Example

A leader who judges that a teacher needs specific and concrete suggestions to deliberate and choose from in the development of a classroom action plan would use the directive-control approach, as described in the previous scenario with Mr. Finer, only up to the postconference. But in the postconference, rather than telling Mr. Finer what to do, the leader would lay out the suggestions in a manner such as this:

Leader: "Here are your options as I see them. First, you could use a threefold attack on these three students by getting them away from each other, giving them individual projects with rewards for work completion, and reminding them what to do. Or you could have conferences with them and their parents or guardians, followed by a daily phone call or a report on their behavior sent home each day. Third, you could line up a personal attention plan to meet with them individually, and apart from each other, where you might gather commitments from each of them as to how they can commit to improving their behavior during class discussion time and what could be done to remind them of their commitment. Fourth, you could make a visit to each student's home, so that a new personal relationship is forged between you and the student and family. Fifth, ..."

After presenting the options, the leader would ask Mr. Finer to tell her, either then or a day or two later, which of the options (either singly, in combination, or in modified form) he will use, and to put in writing the action plan to be implemented.

Discussion: The Directive-Informational Approach

What is of great importance here in distinguishing between the directive-control and the directive-informational approaches is that in the former the leader determines what the action plan will be. In the latter, the teacher determines *within the leader's recommendations* what will be done. This difference between control and information is a fundamental difference in the degree of choice that the teacher has. (Note that the list of behaviors described on pages 62 and 64 applies to both aspects of the directive approach, as does Figure 5.3.)

The Collaborative Approach: An Example

The collaborative approach includes the major behaviors of listening, clarifying, presenting, problem solving, and negotiating. The end result is a mutually agreed upon contract by leader and teacher that delineates the structure, process, and criteria for subsequent instructional improvement. The following example illustrates how the leader and the teacher apply this approach in identifying and solving classroom problems.

Susan Valdock, a 4th grade teacher in a self-contained classroom, is the personification of energy. She is constantly moving around the classroom, talking, listening, and observing. Her classroom is filled with materials, many of which have been created by students and teacher. The classroom has an incessant hum of activity. This fall she has added a new program of technology infusion in literacy instruction. By February, Ms. Valdock appears tired. Twice in one week she has uncharacteristically lost her temper with students. At recess, she stays in her classroom rather than joining others in the teachers lounge.

The collaborative leader might decide to speak casually with Ms. Valdock to see whether she would like help or wait for her to initiate a conversation. In this particular case, the leader is concerned about Ms. Valdock's physical condition. The leader decides that a haggard teacher in an activity-centered room portends trouble. Therefore, the leader decides to take the initiative and meet with the teacher.

Pre-conference

The pre-conference meeting is set for lunch period. Susan and Jon, the leader, bring their lunches and sit casually around a table in the classroom.

Susan: "Well, Jon, how goes it?"

Jon: "Fine. The curriculum study and the technology infusion are taking a lot out of me, but they're progressing. How is life going with you?"

Susan: "Okay. I can't wait until spring vacation, but life is all right."

Jon: "You look tired to me; I'm concerned that you're losing your old vim and vigor."

Susan: "Well, maybe I am a bit tired, but I'll get over it."

Jon: "What can be done to get your energy level back up? What is making you tired?"

Susan: "You know, I've just moved into a new home, and with unpacking boxes, painting walls, getting my own kids adjusted, and trying to keep up with all my classroom activities, it gets to be a bit much. The weekly computer-enhanced student portfolios are really incessant."

Jon: "Well, I can't help you redecorate at home, but maybe I can help you redecorate in class. Maybe you're trying to bite off too much. Your planning has always been a full-time job, and now with the extra chores of moving, maybe you just can't keep up the same pace."

Susan: "I don't feel right about doing less for my students because of my personal life. I'll make it."

Jon: "Yeah, you might make it and spend the last three months of school in a convalescent home. How about if I come into your class over the next few days, just to see what's going on? Maybe we could discuss some ways to do the same for the students in less time."

Susan: "You're always welcome to come in. Don't just observe, though. If you see some students who need help with their activities, please work with them."

Jon: "Okay. For the next week I'll be part-time observer and part-time tutor."

Throughout this pre-conference, friendly negotiation is going on. First, the leader has to gain entry into the teacher's problem. If the teacher did not want help, the leader would have to decide either to back off and try to find access later or to press more forcefully with such words as "I am concerned and feel that as a leader I need to get involved. You appear tired and I want to help." If the teacher still refused, the leader as a negotiator might attempt to counter with a proposal and then look for a counterproposal with such words as "I'm going to come in and take a closer look at your classroom. What do you want me to look at and how do you want to use me in the classroom?" When encountering an unwilling teacher, the leader tries to strike a deal to the effect that the leader's involvement is imperative but asks the teacher to state the conditions for involvement. At this point they can both consider each other's proposals and come to an agreement.

Classroom Observation

As agreed, Jon comes into Susan's classroom over the next four days. He visits for 20 minutes twice each day and is careful to select different periods. During each observation, he keeps a notebook in his hands and moves about the classroom, noting the teacher's instruction, checking on students' activities, discussing with students their assignment, and helping individual students who have questions about their present activities. He jots down notes and, upon leaving the classroom, hurriedly writes down general observations. Here is an example of his notes:

Observation #3, Tuesday, February 15, 10–10:20 a.m.

Students are at three different learning stations. Susan is at the literacy and technology station having individual conferences with children on the latest books they have read. She spends a few minutes asking questions about the books and how students will present a commercial review for a simulated Web site. In the math station, three students are listening to a cassette and filling out worksheets on geometric figures; two other students are estimating the height of the school building. They asked me to guess, and we talked about different ways to mathematically arrive at a good estimate. While talking, we couldn't help noticing the students over in the construction area who were trying to build a miniature lunar craft. The hammer-banging and arguing were quite loud. Susan had to stop her conferences three times to tell the construction group to stop. Finally, she told them to leave the area.

General Impressions

Susan must have an enormous amount of record keeping and assignments to correct each night. There is a bin for collected daily assignments. Also, it seems distracting to students to have noisy activities going on next to quiet activities.

Analysis

After the four days of observations, Jon rereads his notes and jots down questions to ask Susan at the postconference:

1. *How many assignments do you personally correct each day?*
2. *Can you give fewer assignments, or are there alternative ways to correct them?*
3. *What is the reason for three centers?*
4. *Why have so many individual plans?*
5. *Is there another way for students to get feedback on their weekly technology-based reviews?*

Jon, in analyzing his observations, believes that Susan has too much to oversee and coordinate at school—regardless of what she has going on at home. She is doing too much for students and not letting them take more responsibility for their class work. He decides to ask the questions he has written down, listen to Susan's responses, ask her what she thinks could be done, propose what he thinks should be done, and then find mutual solutions to write in a contract form.

Postconference

At the postconference, Jon presents the questions all at once. After listening to the questions, Susan answers that she (1) normally corrects three assignments per student each day (a total of 81); (2) is unsure if fewer assignments could be given because she needs to monitor each student's progress; (3) had considered eliminating the construction center but wanted to keep the art and music centers, which were noisy but not troublesome; (4) did not believe in ability groups and would rather keep the work as individualized as possible; (5) was frustrated about how to save time on the technology portfolios. The leader then carefully begins problem solving by saying, "I think we should take some time to consider what changes you can make to reduce the amount of teacher work and generally streamline your class operation. I have always admired the excitement and interest that you generate in your classroom. Let's not lose that. Tonight, why don't you and I write our own separate lists of two or three possible changes that could be made immediately? Can you meet with me before school tomorrow to share our lists? Say about 7:30?"

That night Jon writes down these ideas:

- *Allow selected students to correct simple assignments.*
- *Conduct more small-group, rather than individual, sessions with students in developing rubrics and guides for how they can critique each other's work.*

The same evening, Susan jots down these ideas:
- *Ask Sonya Jerdel [the 6th grade teacher] if I may use some of her top students as paper checkers and recorders, or see if Felix's mother would like to correct papers. She asked me at the beginning of the year if she might help.*
- *Eliminate the construction center for every day and instead have an all-class construction period on Friday afternoon.*
- *Let the redecorating at home wait until spring vacation; unpacking boxes is enough for now. Stop being so compulsive!*

The following morning, the postconference continues, with the original focus on presenting each other's ideas, followed by revising and choosing activities that both leader and teacher agree will solve the problem of "teacher overload." Let's pick up the conversation after the leader and the teacher have read their suggestions to each other.

Jon: "I don't know about using a parent volunteer or an older student to help correct papers. I think most of your students, if given detailed instructions and a master sheet, could correct spelling assignments. Why don't you let them try it? Or how about group critiques of student work?"

Susan: "It's worth a try for a week or two. Could you help me start this program by helping me develop self-guided rubrics for group assessments?"

Jon: "Sounds fine. I'll help by getting your correctors started. Now what about the idea of silent and active periods and small groups?"

Susan: "No, I don't think so. I want them to learn how to work independently, and they progress so much quicker when I individualize their assignments. I don't want to mess with the basic classroom arrangement right now. I will eliminate the construction center as a daily activity and have it on Friday only."

Jon: "If you don't want to change the basic plan, why eliminate the construction center? Instead, go over the rules for the center and revoke the privilege to use it if students don't obey the rules."

Susan: "Well, that would be one less change to think about."

Jon: "We seem to have come up with a contract. Let's write it down."

Jon writes down what they have agreed to. Susan asks him to also include her promise to herself that she will drop the home decorating until spring break. The leader agrees, and they both sign and date the paper (see Figure 5.4).

5.4

Sample Instruction Contract

Instruction Contract
Between

Ms. Susan Valdock, Teacher
Mr. Jon Gollop, Instructional Lead Teacher
March 18, 2001

Objective: To reduce the amount of teacher work.

Teacher activities:
1. Review portfolios every other week; have students do group reviews of each other on alternate weeks.
2. Stress construction center rules and penalize violators.
3. Postpone home redecorating until spring.

Instructional lead teacher activities:
1. Help develop the self-guided rubrics for group feedback on individual student technology portfolios.
2. Visit classroom and meet with students on the use of the rubrics twice before next meeting.

Follow-up meeting scheduled for April 3, 2001.

_____
Teacher signature

_____
Instructional lead teacher signature

Postcritique

During the next week, Susan and Jon review this process. Susan explains that the procedures have been helpful, because she was truly being pulled into too many directions. She is happy that the leader did not persist with his suggestion for basic classroom reorganization, because she would have felt that her personal life had compromised her professional life. Jon mentions that he is satisfied but hopes that she has not closed her mind to further changes in the classroom.

Discussion: The Collaborative Approach

The leader and the teacher have actively negotiated the plan for action. Neither leader nor teacher has presented a final plan that excludes the other's view. They have reviewed, revised, rejected, proposed, and counterproposed until they could reach agreement. Such a collaborative orientation presupposes that a leader's or a teacher's individual ideas about instructional improvement are not as effective as mutually derived ideas. Each might fight long and hard to promote his or her proposals, but in the end each must accept modifications and adaptations and agree on the necessary actions.

The pragmatic reader might question what would happen if the leader and the teacher could not reach agreement. In a truly collaborative context, a third person, a mediator agreeable to both parties (such as a master teacher or central office consultant), would have to step in with the authority to "break the vote," if it came to that.

The collaborative orientation can be simplified by placing it on the Instructional Leader Behavior Continuum (see Figure 5.5). The final product of the collaboration is a contract, agreed to by both and carried out as a joint responsibility, in the following manner:

5.5

Instructional Leader Behavior Continuum: Collaborative Approach

	1	2	3	4	5	6	7	8	9	10	
T	Listening	Clarifying	Encouraging	Presenting	Problem Solving	Negotiating	Demonstrating	Directing	Standardizing	Reinforcing	**t**
t											**L**
	(c) Leader listens to teacher.	(b) Leader asks teacher to present perceptions of areas for improvement.		(a) Leader presents perceptions of areas for improvement.	(d) Leader and teacher propose alternative actions.	(e) Leader and teacher revise and reject options, and agree on plan.					

Product: Leader and teacher contract

Key:　T = Maximum teacher responsibility　　L = Maximum leader responsibility
　　　　t = Minimum teacher responsibility　　l = Minimum leader responsibility

● **Presenting**—The leader confronts the teacher with his or her perceptions of the instructional area needing improvement.

● **Clarifying**—The leader asks for the teacher's perceptions of the instructional area in question.

● **Listening**—The leader listens to the teacher's perceptions.

● **Problem solving**—The leader and the teacher propose alternative actions for improvement.

● **Negotiating**—The leader and the teacher discuss the options and alter proposed actions until a joint plan is agreed upon.

The Nondirective Approach: An Example

Herbert Klunger walks over to his desk and sits down. He mulls over the English class that has just ended. Members of the class have given oral reports on their interpretation of Shakespeare's Othello. The reports were uninspiring and remarkably uniform in tone and content. Mr. Klunger thinks that many students had either "borrowed" ideas from one student or had bought a summary on Othello and used the main ideas from that publication. Regardless, none of the reports indicated any excitement for the character or for plot development.

Mr. Klunger reflects on previous classes and thinks that students haven't always been this way. One class in particular he remembers: "How they argued and analyzed Shakespeare! If only I could recreate some of that enthusiasm." Later that day Ms. Garcia, his department leader, stops by.

The nondirective orientation rests on the major premise that teachers are capable of analyzing and solving their own instructional problems. When the individual sees the need for change and takes major responsibility for it, instructional improvement is likely to be meaningful and lasting. Therefore, the leader wishes to act as a facilitator for the teacher by imposing little formal structure or direction. This does not mean that the leader is passive, allowing the teacher complete autonomy. Instead, he or she actively uses the behaviors of listening, clarifying, encouraging, and presenting to channel the teacher toward self-discovery. The leader leaves the discovery to the teacher but takes the initiative to see that the necessary self-awareness does develop.

A nondirective leader, more than a collaborative or a directive leader, probably would not use a standard format such as the five steps of clinical supervision when working with a teacher. Instead, depending on the teacher's needs, the leader might simply observe the teacher without analyzing and interpreting, listen without making observations, or arrange inservice training and provide requested materials and resources. For the sake of consistency, however, we will follow the leader-teacher relationship according to the clinical model, noting how the model is altered after the pre-conference. In a nondirective orientation, the teacher determines the steps that will follow the pre-conference.

Pre-conference

Ms. Garcia enters Mr. Klunger's room.

Mr. Klunger: "Welcome, Ms. Garcia. Have a seat. What a class."

Ms. Garcia: "Thank you. Is life treating you all right?"

Mr. Klunger: "Well, I have my ups and downs. At times I think that teaching just isn't for me. The kids have changed so much. Even though state standards say that students must know Shakespeare, the kids don't care. If you are poor, from the 'hood, and concerned about your immediate life, why should you care!?"

Ms. Garcia: "Teaching is not for you? I didn't know you felt that way."

Mr. Klunger: "Yeah, at times I really wonder if I'm accomplishing anything. Just today that 5th period class made Shakespeare appear as exciting as a rotting elm tree. If they can't see the wonder of his writing, I don't know how they can ever appreciate literature."

Ms. Garcia (nodding her head): "It's frustrating."

Mr. Klunger: "Yes, it is!"

Ms. Garcia (pauses, waits for Mr. Klunger to say more. When it appears that Mr. Klunger is not going to speak, she looks attentively at him): "Go on; tell me more about what's so frustrating."

Mr. Klunger: "The students show no initiative. Teaching just isn't exciting anymore. Oh, some of the other classes are tolerable, but that 5th period class is a disaster!"

Ms. Garcia: "What goes on during 5th period?"

Mr. Klunger: "Nothing! That's the problem."

Ms. Garcia: "Nothing?"

Mr. Klunger: "I read them passages of Shakespeare. Ask for their interpretations and try to get a discussion going. They don't identify in any way with this. They think it is all 'old white man' stuff. Maybe if Shakespeare could be a gangsta rapper it would make a difference! I'm sorry, I'm just at a loss."

The conversation continues for 10 more minutes with Mr. Klunger doing most of the talking and Ms. Garcia listening attentively. Finally, after another prolonged pause, Ms. Garcia feels it's time to ask Mr. Klunger for his analysis of what can be done.

Ms. Garcia: "It sounds as though both you and your students are less than happy. What do you think might be done?"

Mr. Klunger: "Obviously my tried-and-true lesson plans for Shakespeare aren't working. I'm going to have to change my approach."

Ms. Garcia: "Do you want to try something different now?"

Mr. Klunger: "Yes, now that I've heard myself whine, I'll stop feeling sorry for myself. Starting tomorrow, I'm going to have a class discussion with them. I'm going to tell them about my dissatisfaction with them and my own teaching and see if we can begin *Macbeth* with a fresh approach. Why don't you come into class and listen to what goes on? You might give me some information that I'm missing."

Ms. Garcia: "Okay. See you tomorrow."

The pre-conference is the "go or no-go" point. If Mr. Klunger did not ask for Ms. Garcia to observe, the process would stop and Ms. Garcia might need to follow up with another conference to discuss what had transpired since their last talk. However, in this case she has been asked to observe informally.

Classroom Observation

For the observation Ms. Garcia enters the classroom, sits in the back, listens to the class discussion, but does not take notes. She notices that Mr. Klunger spends most of the time expressing his disappointment to the students over their lack of interest in Shakespeare. At the end, he does ask them what might be done to improve the class. After much student humor and put-downs, one student states that "the reading is real difficult." Basically, the discussion gets some teacher and student feelings out in the open but fails to solve the problems of either side.

Analysis and Interpretation

Ms. Garcia, returning to her office, thinks Mr. Klunger has not handled the class discussion effectively. Such an approach would never get honest student feedback. She pledges to herself to "bite her lip" and not give advice or suggestions unless Mr. Klunger asks for them. If he asks for her observations, she will merely tell him, without judgments, what she saw. Then she might ask him what he could do to change the content and methods of the lesson to bring Shakespeare to life. If asked for her ideas, she will suggest another classroom discussion to get more student ideas or allowing students to pick out their own passages of *Macbeth* and rewrite them as a modern playwright might. Regardless, at the conclusion of the meeting, she will ask Mr. Klunger what he plans to do and what assistance she might offer.

Postconference

Ms. Garcia enters Mr. Klunger's room during his planning period.

Mr. Klunger (looks up): "Well, didn't I tell you how disinterested those students are? You saw how much response I got—one coherent student reply."

Ms. Garcia: "There was one reply, and the group did seem pretty down."

Mr. Klunger: "They need to get motivated."

Ms. Garcia (jumping on the opening): "How could you get them motivated?"

Mr. Klunger: "Just the question that I was going to ask you."

Ms. Garcia: "You tell me first; then, if you wish, I'll give you my thoughts."

Mr. Klunger: "I think I'm going to have only one class lecure, next week. Instead, I'll introduce *Macbeth,* have them read parts of the entire play, and have them choose one of four scenarios to act out according to their own neighborhood setting. I'll spend time with each group and then on Friday let them give mini-dramas. What do you think?"

Ms. Garcia (being asked, she responds forthrightly): "Sounds fine, but I wonder if all the students would want to act in front of the class. Some of them might feel foolish. Maybe you should ask them for ideas—or I thought they might be assigned different activities, such as drawing a scene, rewriting a section of the play according to modern times, verifying historical circumstances, or putting particular verses to music."

Mr. Klunger: "I like that idea. I'll have four groups focus on the same section of the play, but the groups will be assigned different tasks."

Ms. Garcia: "This certainly will be a change. Maybe you should go slow in doing this, perhaps only two groups to begin with."

Mr. Klunger: "No, I've about had it, but I'm not quitting. I want to get them excited. It's all or nothing! I'm going to start Wednesday when we begin *Macbeth*."

Ms. Garcia: "Can I help you in any way?"

Mr. Klunger: "Could you see if the recent film of *Macbeth* with actors of color is available for rental in three weeks?"

Ms. Garcia: "Will do! What about any help with the class changes?"

Mr. Klunger: "No, thanks—I'm all set."

Ms. Garcia: "Okay, I'll stop by and see how the scene plays out. Good luck!"

Postanalysis

Before the leader leaves the room, she and the teacher have the following exchange:

Mr. Klunger: "Thanks for talking with me. I needed someone to unload my woes on and help me figure out what I was going to do. I'm almost excited again."

Ms. Garcia: "I thought you were troubled about something. I enjoy listening to a scholar thinking out loud. See you later."

Discussion: The Nondirective Approach

Throughout the clinical steps, the teacher was respected as the ultimate determiner of his future course of action (see Figure 5.6). The leader actively listened, rephrased statements, asked questions, and kept the teacher's discourse on track toward resolution. If the teacher had not wanted to change, then the "pure" nondirective leader would have dropped the discussion but would have continued actively at other times to stimulate the teacher to think about what he was doing. In Ms. Garcia's case, her active role turned Mr. Klunger's initial response, "I don't think teaching is for me," to "I'm going to have to change my approach," and eventually to "I'm going to break them into groups and then . . . ." The leader never loses sight of working toward a teacher's self-plan, which might result from borrowed ideas or from teacher insight alone. Nevertheless, the leader accepts the teacher's right and responsibility to make the final decision.

The pragmatic reader might ask, "What if the teacher's plan is downright bad, cruel, or harmful? Does the leader simply acquiesce?" In such a case, the nondirective leader has every right to explain his or her misgivings about the teacher's plan and ask for reconsideration. However, a nondirective orientation assumes that the teacher ultimately makes the wisest and most responsible decisions for his or her own classroom; thus the final determination is still left with the teacher. Please see the discussion on teacher evaluation in Chapter 7 for considerations related to formal teacher evaluations and due process.

Returning to the instructional leader behavior continuum (Figure 5.6), we have seen the nondirective leader engage in listening, encouraging, clarifying, presenting, and problem solving to help the teacher arrive at a self-plan. The following steps represent the simplified proceedings of such actions.

• **Listening**—The leader listens to the teacher's problem by facing and showing attention to the teacher. The leader shows empathy with the teacher by nodding his or her head and restating emotions, such as "It is frustrating."

• **Encouraging**—The leader encourages the teacher to analyze the problem further: "Tell me more," "Please continue on," "Explain that further."

5.6

Instructional Leader Behavior Continuum: Nondirective Approach

T	1	2	3	4	5	6	7	8	9	10	t
	Listening	Clarifying	Encouraging	Presenting	Problem Solving	Negotiating	Demon-strating	Directing	Standard-izing	Reinforcing	L

(a) Leader listens attentively as teacher discusses instructional concern.

(b) Leader encourages teacher to elaborate on concern.

(c) Leader asks questions and rephrases teacher statements to make sure problem is clearly understood.

(d) When asked by teacher, leader offers thoughts and possible solutions.

(e) Leader asks teacher to determine what actions will be taken.

Product: Teacher self-plan

Key: T = Maximum teacher responsibility   L = Maximum leader responsibility
      t = Minimum teacher responsibility   l = Minimum leader responsibility

- **Clarifying**—The leader clarifies the teacher's problem by paraphrasing and questioning: "You mean the students are bored with the topic?" "Do they like anything about the lesson?" "What feedback do you get from them?"
- **Presenting**—If the teacher asks for suggestions, the leader offers alternatives: "The students could be reorganized, or the topic could be changed to include their interests."
- **Problem solving**—Finally, at the moment of truth, the leader asks the teacher to decide on a plan: "What are you going to do?" and offers assistance: "How can I be of help?"

Summary: The Four Approaches

In the *directive-control approach*, the leader emphasizes the behaviors of clarifying, presenting, directing, demonstrating, standardizing, and reinforcing *in developing an assignment for the teacher*. In the *directive-informational approach*, the leader emphasizes clarifying, presenting, directing, demonstrating, standardizing, and reinforcing *in recommending options for the teacher to choose and commit to*. In the *collaborative approach*, the behaviors of presenting, clarifying, listening, problem solving, and negotiating are used to develop a contract between teacher and leader. In the *nondirective approach*, the behaviors of listening, encouraging, clarifying, presenting, and problem solving are used to create a teacher self-plan.

The next chapter explains criteria to determine a teacher's present stage of development so that a leader can be guided in selecting the most appropriate approach. At the end of the chapter, we also return to Ms. Horvback and Mr. Apanka as examples of what might best be done with teachers who display a range of differences.

6

Criteria for Assessing Teacher Competence and Growth

"We propose an audacious goal for America's future—we will provide every student with what should be his/her educational birthright: access to competent, caring, qualified teaching." So states the landmark report of the National Commission on Teaching and America's Future (1996, p. 21).

The report then goes on to describe in detail the competent, caring, qualified professionals who should be in every classroom in every school in America. These are teachers who know well their subjects and content fields; use a variety of appropriate teaching methods and strategies to assess high-quality student learning; understand the developmental needs of their students; and who themselves are active and reflective in the ongoing strengthening of the professional skills of teaching and learning (see Danielson, 1996). Such competent and caring persons can best be attracted to and retained by schools organized to promote continuous learning for all.

So how might instructional leaders apply the four approaches to working with classroom teachers to stretch each individual so that every student will have a competent, caring, qualified teacher?

Please keep in mind as we move into reviewing criteria for determining approaches for working with teachers that nothing is static about teachers or teaching. The thinking and problem-solving skills of teachers, like those of any individuals, are not fixed. People's attitudes and enthusiasm toward their work can and do ebb and flow depending on immediate work conditions and personal concerns. The rhythms, pleasures, and conflicts of adults working with each other are not invariably smooth or rough. What we are soon to delve into are deeper ways of understanding each other, ways to act with each other in a focused and supportive manner and with the overall goal of creating the sense of true teaching—the eternal and fascinating mystery of how to reach all students in more intellectual, powerful, provocative, and personal ways (McDonald, 1992; Palmer, 1998; Ayers, 1993). This eternal mystery is too complex to be solved alone and once and for all, but is so challenging that it must be worked on with friends and colleagues.

Teachers' growth can be viewed in multiple ways; it can be considered in terms of cognition, experience, commitment, identity, and the circumstances of particular students, subject areas, and classrooms. The issue of determining the best ways to work with individual teachers is complex, always an experiment, and needs to be grounded in an overall purpose and direction. Let's begin with simple applications and then increase the complexity.

The Instructional Leader's Overall Direction and Goal

Fostering intellectual and self-motivated growth on the part of teachers means that the instructional leader, whenever possible, uses an approach that demands greater choice and thought on the part of the teacher.

A directive-control approach, in which the source of thoughts and actions to be taken comes unilaterally from the leader, should be used only in an emergency situation in which a teacher is overwhelmed, paralyzed, totally inexperienced, or incompetent in the current classroom situation. In essence, such controlled assignments have as their goal to save the students by keeping the teacher from drowning in a sea of ineffectual practice.

A directive-informational approach is used in a minimal way to begin to push initiative from the leader to the teacher by asking the teacher to choose among specific alternatives. The generation of observations and ideas from the teacher can come quickly after a successful round or rounds of directive-informational interventions.

A collaborative approach is most often the desired choice in schools that promote learning as cooperative and collegial. Both leader and teacher approach the tasks of improvement as a meeting of equals, trying to generate together the best course of future actions. This approach demands a respectful, egalitarian relationship.

A nondirective approach is best used when teachers themselves clearly have greater knowledge and understanding of their teaching than does the leader. The leader's critical role is not to leave such masterful teachers alone but to facilitate their own thinking and improvement plan and to provide resources that assist in the attainment of the plan.

So, in a linear sweep, the direction of all "up-close" work with teachers is, regardless of the initial intervention, to move toward collaborative and, at times, nondirective approaches as quickly as possible (see Figure 6.1). We don't want teacher leaders to foster dependency relationships. We want each teacher to be autonomous and competent.

Determining whether a teacher is best served by a particular approach can be accomplished by (1) seeing how much initiative, thought, and action the person already takes in looking at his or her own

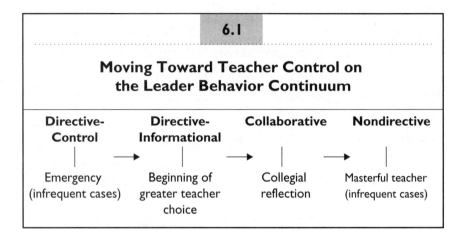

6.1

Moving Toward Teacher Control on the Leader Behavior Continuum

Directive-Control	Directive-Informational	Collaborative	Nondirective
Emergency (infrequent cases)	Beginning of greater teacher choice	Collegial reflection	Masterful teacher (infrequent cases)

teaching and learning; and (2) reviewing the different approaches with the teacher, clarifying which one will be used and why, and then later reviewing with the teacher how useful the chosen approach was and which alternative might be more appropriate for the next cycle of work.

Teachers' Developmental Characteristics

For teacher leaders, it is helpful to think about the optimal level of two factors in a teacher's development. The first is the teacher's commitment to his or her own teaching and to student learning, and the second is the teacher's level of abstraction.

Commitment

Educators indicate that some teachers make a tremendous commitment to teaching, in terms of time and emotion, and some make little or no commitment. Teachers who have no commitment are viewed as caring only about themselves, simply going through the motions to keep a job, not caring about improving or being willing to give time and energy to look at possible ways of improving. Teachers of moderate commitment might work in spurts, or single out one particular academic area to work hard on while neglecting others, or work diligently with a particular group of students and spend less time with others. Teachers of high commitment constantly want to do more for their students and other students and to help colleagues far beyond the contracted hours of the job. Figure 6.2 shows levels of teachers' commitment.

Abstraction

Teachers who are functioning with low abstract thinking skills may not be sure whether they have a classroom problem, or, if they are aware of a problem, they are very confused about it. They aren't sure what can be done, and they typically need to be shown what can be done. They normally exhibit a limited repertoire of one or two solutions, such as "be tougher" or "give more homework," regardless of whether the problem involves misbehavior, underachievement, or inappropriate textbooks.

Teachers with moderate abstract thinking skills can usually define the problem according to how they see it. They can think of one or two

6.2		
Levels of Teachers' Commitment		
Low	**Moderate**	**High**
• Little concern for students	• Some concern for students	• High concern for students and other teachers
• Little time or energy expended	• Energy expended sporadically or only in certain areas	• Extra time and energy expended
• Primary concern with keeping one's job	• Primary concern varies according to circumstances	• Primary concern with doing more for others

possible actions but have difficulty in coordinating an overall plan. For example, if many students in a chemistry class are failing, teachers of moderate abstract thinking skills might think of creating some remedial packets written at a lower reading level. They might then implement the packets with students but fail to plan ahead for such matters as monitoring progress, allotting enough class time, providing other work for the more advanced students, explaining the rules for using the packets, and clarifying the need for more individualized work. The moderately abstract teacher might face these additional issues as they occur without having planned preventive measures.

Teachers with high abstract thinking skills can view the problem from many perspectives (their own, students', parents', aides', administrators') and can generate many alternative solutions. They can think through the advantages and disadvantages of each plan and decide upon the most promising one. They are willing to change that plan if the predicted consequences do not materialize. When planning, they can judge additional problems that might arise and systematically provide prevention before trouble occurs. Figure 6.3 highlights the characteristics of varying levels of teachers' abstract thinking.

Intersecting Variables to Establish Criteria

Using the two variables of *level of commitment* and *level of abstraction*, the instructional leader can assess an individual teacher's status and use that information to select an effective approach. The assessment can be accomplished with a simple figure showing two intersecting lines—a horizontal *line of commitment* (ranging from "low" at the left to "high" at the right) and a vertical *line of abstraction* (ranging from "low" at the bottom to "high" at the top). As seen in Figure 6.4, the resulting four quadrants define "types" of teachers.

6.3		
Levels of Teachers' Abstract Thinking		
Low	**Moderate**	**High**
● Confused about the problem	● Can define the problem	● Can think of the problem from many perspectives
● Doesn't know what can be done	● Can think of one or two possible responses to the problem	● Can generate many alternative plans
● "Show me"	● Has trouble thinking through a comprehensive plan	● Can choose a plan and think through each step

Quadrant I: Teacher Dropouts. These teachers have both a low level of commitment and a low level of abstraction. They simply go through the minimal motions in order to keep the job. They have little motivation for improving their competencies. Furthermore, they cannot think about what changes could be made and are quite satisfied to keep the same routine day after day. They do not see any reasons for improvement. They blame causes of any difficulties on others. In their view, it is the students or the administration or the community that need help, never the teacher. They come to work exactly on time and leave school as soon as officially permissible.

Quadrant II: Unfocused Workers. These teachers have a high level of commitment but a low level of abstraction. They are enthusiastic, energetic, and full of good intentions. They want to become better

6.4

Four "Types" of Teachers

High

Abstraction

Quadrant III
Analytical Observers

Quadrant IV
Professionals

Low ——————— *Level of Commitment* ——————— High

Quadrant I
Teacher Dropouts

Level of

Quadrant II
Unfocused Workers

Low

teachers and make their classes more exciting and relevant to students. They work very hard and usually leave school staggering under materials to be worked on at home. Unfortunately, though, their good intentions are thwarted by their lack of ability to think problems through and then to act fully and realistically. They usually get involved in multiple projects and activities but become easily confused, discouraged, and swamped by self-imposed and unrealistic tasks. As a result, rarely do these teachers complete any particular instructional improvement effort before undertaking a new one.

Quadrant III: Analytical Observers. These teachers have a low level of commitment but a high level of abstraction. These teachers are the intelligent, highly verbal people who are always full of great ideas about what can be done in their own classrooms, in other classrooms, and in the school as a whole. They can discuss the issues clearly and think through the steps necessary for successful implementation. This type is labeled Analytical Observers because their ideas often do not result in any action. They know what needs to be done but are unwilling to commit the time, energy, and care necessary to carry out the plan.

Quadrant IV: Professionals. These teachers have both a high level of commitment and a high level of abstraction. They are the true Professionals, committed to continually improving themselves, their students, and their fellow faculty members. They can think about the task at hand, consider alternatives, make a rational choice, and develop and carry out an appropriate plan of action. Not only can they do this for their classrooms but with the faculty as a whole. Others regard them as informal leaders, people to whom others go willingly for help. Not only do these teachers provide ideas, activities, and resources, but they become actively involved in seeing any proposed plan through to its completion. They are both thinkers and doers.

By focusing on the two variables of *level of commitment* and *level of abstraction* that are related to teacher effectiveness, the instructional leader can think about individual teachers as developmentally different. Then the leader can work with teachers in ways to help them develop higher levels of abstraction and higher levels of commitment. The leader must first begin to work with teachers at their current stage on each of these levels. As gains are made, the leader can provide less direction and foster more teacher autonomy.

With such a scheme, the leader can determine a starting point for using the interpersonal leadership approaches with individual teachers. The Teacher Dropout is matched with the directive-control approach; the Unfocused Worker is matched with the directive-informational approach with emphasis on presenting leader ideas; the Analytical Observer is matched with the collaborative approach with emphasis on negotiating; and the Professional is best matched with mostly collaborative and nondirective approaches.

A word of caution here: the two variables of abstraction and commitment, the four categories of teachers' skills, and the alignments with particular approaches are helpful lenses for understanding and determining ways for working with teachers, but they are somewhat limited in application. First, people don't fall neatly into simple categories. Second, there is complexity within the same teacher—he or she may be an Unfocused Worker when teaching mathematics and a Professional when teaching science in the gifted and talented program. Third, many subjective and interpersonal factors cloud or clarify assessments of one person by another. And fourth, the bottom line is not necessarily the outward manifestations of thought and time but rather how well students are being served.

Diversity and Development in Working with Teachers

In my earlier work (Glickman, 1980), my discussion of these concepts of development of commitment and abstraction and the visual four-quadrant scheme was not so much wrong as it was incomplete. Obviously, we cannot account for and understand everything in working with another person. We would never get around to action. But as I look back, I see a danger in over-looking the social and professional factors of status, power, hierarchy, and influence, and the identity factors of race, ethnicity, gender, socioeconomic class, and life histories (Delpit, 1994; Robinson & Howard-Hamilton, 2000). That's why I am discussing these factors further here.

Suppose a young, female, lesbian, Ph.D., fifth-generation Latino American instructional leader in her second year of teaching is working with an older, male, heterosexual, first-generation Asian American with 42 years of teaching experience in the same school. Does it make sense that she might face a different set of complexities than if she were working with someone of her own background, lifestyle, and culture? This is not to say that differences will necessarily predict the develop-ment of more difficult—or more congenial—reciprocal relations, but to emphasize that awareness of ethnic, cultural, and age-related differences is an important consideration in determining entry points for discus-sions about observations of teaching and learning.

In another example, a young, white, male instructional leader might inadvertently be seen as disrespectful by an older teacher of color if he refers to that teacher on a casual first-name basis or gives out directives that may be interpreted as asserting "the man." The same may be true of a leader who inadvertently slips into informal, judgmental comments about the poor or the "rednecks" to a teacher who grew up in a poor, rural, working-class region. Or the leader who begins school faculty cel-ebrations with public prayers in the name of Jesus or plans elaborate Christmas celebrations at which the individual Muslim, Jew, Hindu, or agnostic feels diminished. The idea is not that a leader must be self-con-scious or politically correct about everything said or done, but that it is important to realize that an honest, reciprocal, professional relation means finding out more about the lives, aspirations, and hopes of others

(Young & Laible, 2000; Robinson & Howard-Hamilton, 2000). For additional information on professional development and practice in understanding cultural, ethnic, and personal identity, please see the list of Resources near the end of the book.

To apply this discussion to the analysis made possible by Figure 6.4, a leader might conclude that a teacher has a low level of abstraction because she does not verbally analyze a situation, when in actuality she is exhibiting cultural values that emphasize the need to remain quiet and respectful. Similarly, what might appear to be a low level of school commitment may have nothing to do with caring about one's own students; it could stem from a teacher's feelings of rejection and disrespect generated within the school.

Ms. Horvback and Mr. Apanka

Now let's return to the two teachers, Ms. Horvback and Mr. Apanka, introduced in Chapter 4. How should one go about working with the experienced teacher, Ms. Horvback of New Castle High, or the younger Mr. Apanka of Rural Elementary? They differ in age, position, experience, subject, race/ethnicity, and teaching level. Reading descriptions on pieces of paper, we really don't know either one as a person, just that they are different people, have different roles in their schools, and are in different career phases. But now, in a general sense, let's apply some approaches to the concerns and needs of these teachers.

The way to work with either one is to begin in a collegial manner—whether in clinical supervision, peer coaching, critical friends, or action research structures. It is also important to assume that each teacher is committed, thoughtful, and has aspirations and ideas about improving learning for students. A collaborative approach—in sharing and articulating learning goals, in determining the focus of observation and student work, in sharing feedback and brainstorming ideas and actions, and in jointly creating an action plan—should be the first concern. If Mr. Apanka turns out to have much more expertise and enthusiasm for teaching than many beginners, the leader might, over time, move toward a nondirective approach (Gordon, 1991). If in a collaborative conference Ms. Horvback uses her age and experience to resist the suggestion that she needs to work on learning goals compatible with the school and the learning standards expected of all students, the leader might, over time, move to a directive-informational approach. If she still shows no initiative, and with further documentation of a lack of progress in adapting to children's needs, a directive-control approach might be appropriate.

Each teacher in each classroom is unique. Talent, energy, thought, and knowledge are not the purview of any one group. This explanation is meant to convey that working with teachers to improve instruction is always an experiment, a trial-and-error research cycle of finding out what structures, formats, and observations best support the growth of individual competence, improved student learning, and overall school success.

7

Purpose, Strength, and Collegial Force
for School Success

One principal, a personal friend whom I had called to discuss some school issues, exclaimed that after three years of perseverance toward becoming one of the most successful schools in a large district, "we finally had our last naysayer go. She came into my office on Monday and told me that she just couldn't work in our school any longer. She couldn't stand it that everyone knew what everyone else was doing in the classrooms. She wanted to be in a place where she could be alone to teach by herself and not be bothered by the eyes and ideas of others." The principal added that she was happy for this teacher and very happy for the future of the school. After three years of clinical work, peer coaching, and study groups, all those not willing to work and assist others were now gone. This story may seem harsh, but my friend is not an uncaring principal. She is truly admired by faculty as a colleague and one of the kindest and fairest persons anyone could ever work with.

What this story illustrates is the reality of what is involved in improving a school so that it becomes the best possible place for students. This school, one of 40 in the district and with a more economically and ethnically diverse population than most, had risen to be among the top schools in overall achievement. Student rates of literacy had more than doubled. To be serious about the typical slogan "All students can learn" means that the word "all" must be defined and the word "learn" must be specified. These achievements can happen only by critique, dialogue, and common work. The principal in this school works in classrooms as a substitute to release teachers for peer coaching; she participates in several critical friends groups; and she shares authority with students, faculty, staff, parents, and businesspersons. The work of school improvement is not a glory train; people disagree with each other, they get tired, and unpredictable negatives occur. But when all is said and done, students learn well, staff and faculty want to be there, and parents are proud of the education provided.

Leaders live with the very expectations they have for others, being open and willing to be scrutinized as to how well they carry on their own professional work. Those educators who can't publicly practice the act of continuous improvement over time must either leave of their own will, transfer to a different setting, or be terminated. Clearly this is not easy work.

Renewing Classrooms and Schools

Let's return to the idea that a focus on classroom teaching and learning is part and parcel of overall school renewal efforts. Refer to Figure 7.1, first introduced in Chapter 1 and reproduced here.

First, let's look at the center of the concentric circles in the figure—the target. The bull's-eye of all classroom and school efforts, represented by Circle A, is to enhance quality student learning that gives every child, regardless of race, ethnicity, gender, class, or disability, the

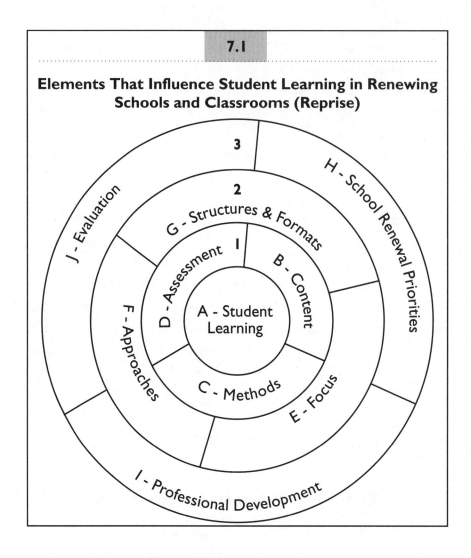

7.1

Elements That Influence Student Learning in Renewing Schools and Classrooms (Reprise)

knowledge, skills, and understandings needed to become a valued and valuable member of a vital democratic society. This is the primary goal of every school with public purpose (see Glickman, 1998). Moving to Concentric Circle 1 immediately surrounding the center, we see that student learning is directly related to Segment B, the content taught; Segment C, the instructional methods used; and Segment D, the assessment strategies employed.

Now let's concentrate on Concentric Circle 2. To improve the quality of classroom teaching, there must be ongoing attention to Segment E, a focus by every teacher on learning goals, observations, and student work; Segment F, interpersonal approaches (directive-control, directive-informational, collaborative, and nondirective) used with the teacher to work directly on classroom teaching and learning; and Segment G, structures and formats for clinical supervision, peer coaching, critical friends, and action research/study groups with scheduled times and facilitation.

To bring utmost coherence and power to teaching and learning, changes in instruction must be an ongoing element in a comprehensive school change/improvement/renewal process, represented by Concentric Circle 3. This circle includes Segment H, overall schoolwide-instructional goals and priorities; Segment I, school-based professional development expected of every faculty member; and Segment J, formative and summative evaluation of improved learning for all students.

The purpose of Figure 7.1 is to show the various classroom and school contexts for improving student learning and, eventually, achieving the overall mission of the school. Of course, this graphic representation oversimplifies the complexities of endeavors to improve learning—it's simply a method for letting you, the reader, see the figurative forest without all those trees in the way. The complexities do not go away, but it is helpful to look at this visual overview, especially for checking your own school or district efforts to see if they are sufficiently comprehensive. Comprehensive efforts, with careful attention paid to *all* the elements of the process, promise the greatest rewards and benefits in student learning.

Another matter of great importance is the formal evaluation process required by states and districts for the assessment of the professional performance of teachers. The following section provides guidance for how the formal process relates to the approaches offered in this book.

Teacher Evaluation

Teachers, like all individuals, should be treated with dignity, respect, and confidence—the same way that all students should be treated. An atmosphere of ridicule, gossip, belittling, and arrogant power has no place in schools that purport to be public, with the mission of preparing students for the life of a democracy. All teachers, whether young or old, extraordinarily competent or staggeringly inept, deserve systematic support and assistance to change, grow, improve, and share.

It is best to separate the direct assistance for continuous improvement from the formal summative school district or state evaluations for tenure, contract continuation, and contract renewal. It is easier for people to open up about the real struggles and difficulties of their own classroom teaching to a person who has no role in the formal summative evaluation. For these reasons, I have suggested that formal evaluation and professional development processes be separated by using some of the following strategies (Glickman, 1987).

• **Annually, separate competent teachers from marginal teachers through evaluations completed by late fall.** The evaluator uses a standard, uniform evaluation instrument to make an initial judgment, after one full cycle of observations, as to which teachers are competent and which are questionable. The questionable teachers are placed on a "needs improvement" plan that details what changes they need to make in order to reach satisfactory performance in the next evaluation cycle. An experienced teacher or specialist is assigned to work with the teacher on the improvement efforts. Teachers who are judged as competent after the first cycle are asked to establish their own instructional classroom goals and professional growth plans. Further cycles of observations and conferences are no longer tied to evaluation but rather to feedback about their growth plans.

- **Establish a two-track, three-year program of two cycles of observations and conferences per year for all teachers.** In Track 1, teachers are observed by an evaluator in accordance with a standard evaluation form, used throughout the school system for contract-renewal purposes. Teachers judged satisfactory after the first cycle of observation move into Track 2, which focuses on professional development and instructional improvement. Observations for the remainder of the three years are focused on enhancing competence. Track 2 involves three phases leading to the development of an instructional professional development plan. In Track 2, no rating scales are kept, nor are formal records kept or reported to any party. Teachers who do not pass the first cycle of Track 1 remain in Track 1 until they satisfy the required evaluation, or they are removed from employment.

- **Divide the process so that the evaluation procedures and the professional development process can occur simultaneously but are viewed as discrete from each other.** One method for an instructional improvement sequence is to have each teacher choose an instructional improvement goal and select the sources of assistance he or she believes will be most helpful in achieving the goal—clinical supervision, peer coaching, critical friends, or a study group. The teacher discusses the year's direct-assistance plan with a designated coordinator (school principal, department head, or team leader) and arranges visiting schedules. The normal contract evaluation process conducted by the designated evaluator continues throughout the year, separate from the instructional improvement process.

- **Establish separate roles for evaluators and professional development facilitators.** In some school districts, central office supervisors conduct all formal evaluations, and the principals provide instructional improvement assistance. More often, it is the other way around: principals conduct evaluations and central office or school-based personnel (master teachers, lead teachers, department heads, assistant principals, or peers) provide assistance. In either case, one position is clearly delineated as a staff position, concerned with assisting teachers; the other is designated as a line position, concerned with evaluating teachers.

• **Integrate direct assistance with school-based professional development conducted by peers and trainers.** The focus for inservice education developed by the staff can become the focus for direct assistance. Meanwhile, the regular evaluation process remains intact. For example, a school decides to study and employ a new instructional model (cooperative learning, mastery learning, or cognitive monitoring, for example) for improving certain student learning goals. As part of teachers' professional growth, they individually set goals on what they plan to do to implement the model; then each teacher receives a minimum of two cycles of observations and conferences from peers or trainers to refine or expand his or her skills. Such communication is kept confidential between teachers and assistors. The official school evaluator continues to conduct the district evaluation to judge overall teacher competence.

• **Redefine evaluation between evaluators and teachers.** Many states and districts require an annual evaluation and summarized report on each teacher, completed by an officially designated, school-based evaluator. Yet some states or districts do not define the content or purpose of the evaluation. In such cases a district committee, a school council, or an individual evaluator and teacher can define at the outset the types of evaluation to be done. Will it be a summative evaluation to determine competence or a formative evaluation to promote professional growth? Any of the five previously listed procedures, or a combination thereof, might be used, along with the terminology of formative and summative evaluations, to conform to the mandated requirements for annual evaluations of all employees.

In all cases, involvement in continuous improvement of classroom teaching and learning through the opening up of one's classroom and the review of student work with others should be an essential component of the formal summative evaluation process. In other words, participation in continuous improvement is part of the evaluation; the particular nature of the interactions, discussions, and specific plans is not.

If, after repeated formal evaluations and provisions of assistance and resources, a teacher is still unable to meet the learning needs of his or her students, the evaluator must consider moving toward termination of the teacher's contract. The evaluator must ensure that this judgment is not influenced by personal bias toward the individual and must be able to secure corroborating, documented evidence by others. Under such circumstances, the following information for proceeding toward termination of the teacher's contract is useful. John Dayton, a scholar of constitutional law related to public education, explains:

> Related to teacher evaluation, the primary concern is one of due process. The 5th Amendment and the 14th Amendment of the U.S. Constitution require adequate due process whenever government actions significantly impinge on "life, liberty, or property." Liberty and property may be significantly impinged upon by the actions of government officials (public school employees) in the evaluation process.

> In regard to liberty, the U.S. Supreme Court noted in *Board of Regents v. Roth*, 408 U.S. 564 (1972), when government actions "might seriously damage (a teacher's) standing and associations in (the teacher's) community: that individual is entitled to adequate due process." Due process includes at a minimum notice of the proposed action, a presentation of the evidence this action is based upon, and the opportunity for a hearing on the proposed action. The Court has noted that: "Where a person's good name, reputation, honor, or integrity is at stake because of what the government is doing to him, notice and an opportunity to be heard are essential." The other protected interest is

a property interest: Untenured teachers only have a property interest in the defined term of their current contract (from August to May, for example). Nonetheless, if nontenured teachers are fired or demoted prior to the expiration of that contract period, the government has impinged on a protected property right.

Further, if officials make stigmatizing comments about the employee in the dismissal process, they may impinge on a protected liberty interest. This is why school board attorneys typically instruct school administrators to simply send a notice of nonrenewal and to avoid any further comment on the matter. Note, though, that making negative comments in formative evaluations, that are not publicly circulated, generally does not impinge on a protected liberty interest. However, when school officials repeat these same charges later in a summative and public nonrenewal context, this may constitute an impingement on protected liberty interests.

The difference between tenure and nontenure is that tenured persons have a continuing contractual right rather than a periodic one. Therefore, any time tenured persons are dismissed, the government is impinging on a property right, and due process is required (notice and hearing).

Although these due process protections are required by the federal Constitution, state law governs the specific procedures concerning due process and teacher dismissal. (J. Dayton, personal communication, May 23, 2000, quoted with permission)

A school leader always should exhibit empathy and care throughout a dismissal process. The personal toil is burdensome, but the task of removing, or counseling out of the field, an uncaring, unmotivated, or terribly disorganized person from the teaching field is a plus for the future of the students and the other professionals in the school. In the end, it often is a plus for the dismissed teacher finally to be relieved of a job that he or she has proven, over time, to be incapable of carrying out.

To Conclude: Where to Take Action, as a School

Now, as this book draws to an end, let me suggest ways to use the structures, formats, and approaches in a comprehensive way to move a school forward. Think about the four approaches to working with teachers: nondirective, collaborative, directive-informational, and directive-control. In a school full of faculty who are self-starters, who are resourceful and curious, and who work well professionally, much of what has been outlined in this book probably is already taking place. A nondirective approach by the principal or other formal school leader(s) for letting the faculty lead and develop their formats and structures further would be the appropriate approach.

In a school with a common history of fragmented efforts to improve but little open and visible collaboration among teachers to see each other at work or to review the work of each other's students, a collaborative approach would be appropriate. In this case, a brainstorming session for all members could include discussions on ways to provide focus, structure, and time for "up-close" work, followed by a schoolwide decision-making process (see Glickman, 1993; Allen et al., 1999).

In a school with a lack of common learning goals across departments or grade levels and teachers working mostly in private, a directive-informational approach would be appropriate. To begin the cross-fertilization of ideas, observations, and actions, the leader could lay out some of the options for continuous improvement as part of everyone's professional development (either clinical supervision, peer coaching, critical friends, or study/action research group) and then ask faculty members to choose their desired process.

Finally, in a school marked by isolation, routine, privacy, stagnation or decline in the achievement of students, and resistance to individual or collective change, a directive-control orientation requiring faculty to be in a continuous improvement program is necessary. Such schools might have high aggregate achievement scores that mask serious inequities of particular subgroups of students by income, ethnicity, race, gender, or disability. Schools where faculty are smugly satisfied with their current teaching (and thus blame students, parents, and external conditions for any low achievement) correlate with stagnation and decline. Competent teachers and powerful schools know that when it comes to education—no matter how well or poorly one is currently doing—one must always learn how to be better (Lieberman & Miller, 2001).

In all these scenarios, the direction of leadership and development of schoolwide instructional change is a shift of responsibility for growth from supervisor to supervisee, from master teacher to mentee, from teacher to student. And so it is with continuous improvement. No matter which approach one uses to intervene—directive-control, directive-informational, collaborative, or nondirective—the aim is always toward more individual autonomy for achieving collective learning goals. In Figure 7.2, you'll find guiding questions, correlated to Figure 7.1, to use in determining the next steps for your school. Please think through these questions by yourself or with others as you devise your plan. If thought out carefully, with the possibility of ongoing adjustments, your plan will alter the nature of teaching, improve the quality of learning, and move your school, your professionalism, and education itself to a higher and more satisfying plateau.

Let's End as We Began

How does one's teaching get better? What happens that increases student learning? As we have asked ourselves these questions and looked at teachers, classrooms, and schools, we might now have a better set of knowledge, skills, practices, tools, and understandings. At the beginning, I wrote that the answer was really quite simple. As teachers, we have to step out of the privacy of our own work and publicly open ourselves to the critiques of others.

7.2

Guiding Questions

1. What are our schoolwide learning goals? How did we arrive at them and how do we use them? (Segment H)

2. What is our professional development plan for every single faculty member, congruent with schoolwide learning goals? How does the plan open everyone's classroom teaching and student learning to the scrutiny of others? (Segment I)

3. How do we assess the overall progress that we are making on schoolwide student learning goals? (Segment J)

4. What is the focus on teaching and learning that every teacher will take in developing his or her own classroom goals? (Segment E)

5. What structures (clinical supervision, peer coaching, critical friends, action research/study groups, others) and what formats (observation, instruments, student work/test scores, completed assignments, performances, demonstrations, portfolios, culmination projects) will be used? (Segment G)

6. What approaches will we use in working with each other (nondirective, collaborative, directive-informational, directive-control)? (Segment F)

7. What changes will each teacher make in assessments of student learning? (Segment D)

8. What changes will each teacher make in teaching methods? (Segment C)

9. What changes will each teacher make in content taught? (Segment B)

Speaking for myself, I acknowledge that any success I have had as a teacher does not belong to me alone. For example, when confronting a class of 300 students for the first time, I spent the semester beforehand observing and talking with a colleague 15 years younger than I who showed me how to organize and direct such large groups. I borrowed—or stole—everything he did in that class. I copied him until I became secure in the routines and then began to modify them to suit my hunches.

Several years later, teaching a different course, I was not happy with the quality of student work in my class, so I went across campus to another faculty member in a discipline other than mine, a person whom I hardly knew but who had a reputation as a great organizer of student work. He agreed to a semester-long peer-coaching relationship with me. We observed in each other's classrooms, shared feedback, and conducted an action research study from a sample of each other's students. I changed my syllabus, altered my activities, and reformatted discussions according to what I learned from him.

Five years later, when having students give public demonstrations of their work as culminating exams, I visited and worked with classrooms and faculty in another region of the country for 10 days to learn how to develop and use standards and rubrics of student work.

My point is simple. I have been a teacher at institutions with supportive colleagues and with leaders who have provided time, resources, and structures to help us in the eternal professional discovery—the discovery and recognition of student capabilities, and the discovery and recognition of the art and science of reaching them. Without others, I cannot learn. And if I cannot learn, I cannot teach.

Ultimately, the job of all educational leaders is to help me excel with my students so, in turn, I can be a source of assistance to other colleagues in achieving the dreams of our school and our profession. To challenge students to achieve a valued life beyond what anyone could ever imagine is why we teach and why schools exist. Leadership for the improvement of classroom teaching and learning is the essential force for making our dreams come true.

Appendix A:

Peer Coaching Forms

Pre-conference Log (to be filled out by coach)

Date of pre-conference: _____

Teacher code number: _____

Coach code number: _____

Lesson background:

- What subject will the teacher be teaching when observed?

- What is the purpose of the lesson that will be observed?

- Observation:

- What is the reason and purpose for the observation?

- What is the specific focus of the observation?

- How will the observation be recorded?

Date of observation: _____

Location of observation: _____

Time of observation: _____

Date of postconference: _____

Location of postconference: _____

Time of postconference: _____

Plan for Instructional Improvement

Date of postconference: _____

Time of postconference: _____

Teacher code number: _____

Coach code number: _____

Objective to be worked on:

Activities to be undertaken to achieve objective:

Resources needed:

Date of next pre-conference: _____

Time of next pre-conference: _____

Teacher's Perceptions of Peer Coaching Cycle

Teacher code number: _____

Coach code number: _____

Describe the peer coaching cycle in which you just participated:

How much time would you estimate was spent on the entire coaching cycle?

- Pre-observation conference: _____
- Teaching the lesson: _____
- Postobservation conference: _____

What do you think about the coaching process in which you just participated? Why do you think that way?

What went particularly well in the coaching process?

What did not go as well as you would have liked in the coaching process?

Will the coaching process in which you just participated result in a change in the way you teach? If not, why not? If so, how?

If you participated in another cycle of peer coaching, what would you do differently?

Coach's Perceptions of Peer Coaching Cycle

Teacher code number: _____

Coach code number: _____

Describe the peer coaching cycle in which you just participated:

How much time would you estimate was spent on each phase of the coaching cycle?

- Pre-observation conference:_____
- Developing the observation instrument:_____
- Observing the lesson:_____
- Analyzing the lesson taught:_____
- Writing up the analysis:_____
- Postobservation Conference: _____

What do you think about the coaching process in which you just participated? Why do you think that way?

What went particularly well in the coaching process?

What did not go as well as you would have liked in the coaching process?

Will the coaching process in which you just participated result in a change in the way you teach? If not, why not? If so, how?

If you participated in another cycle of peer coaching, what would you do differently?

Appendix B:

Frameworks for Teaching—A Focus for Observations

The following appendix consists of three parts: B1, Charlotte Danielson's Components of Professional Practice; B-2, an excerpt from the California Standards for the Teaching Profession; and B-3, the Continuum for Assessing Student Learning from the Santa Cruz New Teacher Project/New Teacher Center.

The Danielson work is offered as an example of domains of teaching and learning to find a common focus and illustrate how that focus can be broken into components to guide observations and group work. Likewise, the excerpt from the California Standards provides indicators for how and what teachers might think about in collecting data and making progress on a particular professional practice. Finally, the Santa Cruz materials provide a rubric of teacher development (from "beginning" to "innovating") that can be used for self-analysis, peer coaching, supervising, and group critique.

All of these examples are intended to provide the reader with, first, a wide lens for viewing teaching and learning and, second, a narrower set of indicators and rubrics for specific observations and data collection.

Appendix B-1: Components of Professional Practice

Domain 1: Planning and Preparation

Component 1a: *Demonstrating Knowledge of Content and Pedagogy*
   Knowledge of content
   Knowledge of prerequisite relationships
   Knowledge of content-related pedagogy

Component 1b: *Demonstrating Knowledge of Students*
   Knowledge of characteristics of age group
   Knowledge of students' varied approaches to learning
   Knowledge of students' skills and knowledge
   Knowledge of students' interests and cultural heritage

Component 1c: *Selecting Instructional Goals*
   Value
   Clarity
   Suitability for diverse students
   Balance

Component 1d: *Demonstrating Knowledge of Resources*
   Resources for teaching
   Resources for students

Component 1e: *Designing Coherent Instruction*
   Learning activities
   Instructional materials and resources
   Instructional groups
   Lesson and unit structure

Component 1f: *Assessing Student Learning*
   Congruence with instructional goals
   Criteria and standards
   Use for planning

(continued)

Appendix B-1: Components of Professional Practice (continued)

Domain 2: The Classroom Environment

Component 2a: *Creating an Environment of Respect and Rapport*

    Teacher interaction with students

    Student interaction

Component 2b: *Establishing a Culture for Learning*

    Importance of the content

    Student pride in work

    Expectations for learning and achievement

Component 2c: *Managing Classroom Procedures*

    Management of instructional groups

    Management of transitions

    Management of materials and supplies

    Performance of noninstructional duties

    Supervision of volunteers and paraprofessionals

Component 2d: *Managing Student Behavior*

    Expectations

    Monitoring of student behavior

    Response to student misbehavior

Component 2e: *Organizing Physical Space*

    Safety and arrangement of furniture

    Accessibility to learning and use of physical resources

Domain 3: Instruction

Component 3a: *Communicating Clearly and Accurately*

    Directions and procedures

    Oral and written language

Component 3b: *Using Questioning and Discussion Techniques*

    Quality of questions

    Discussion techniques

    Student preparation

Component 3c: *Engaging Students in Learning*

    Representation of content

    Activities and assignments

    Grouping of students

    Instructional materials and resources

    Structure and pacing

Component 3d: *Providing Feedback to Students*

    Quality: accurate, substantive, constructive, and specific

    Timeliness

Component 3e: *Demonstrating Flexibility and Responsiveness*

    Lesson adjustment

    Response to students

    Persistence

(continued)

Appendix B-1: Components of Professional Practice (continued)

Domain 4: Professional Responsibilities

Component 4a: *Reflecting on Teaching*

    Accuracy

    Use in future teaching

Component 4b: *Maintaining Accurate Records*

    Student completion of assignments

    Student progress in learning

    Noninstructional records

Component 4c: *Communicating with Families*

    Information about the instructional program

    Information about individual students

    Engagement of families in the instructional program

Component 4d: *Contributing to the School and District*

    Relationships with colleagues

    Service to the school

    Participation in school and district projects

Component 4e: *Growing and Developing Professionally*

    Enhancement of content knowledge and pedagogical skill

    Service to the profession

Component 4f: *Showing Professionalism*

    Service to students

    Advocacy

Appendix B-2: Assessing Learning
(An Excerpt from the California Standards for the Teaching Profession)

Standard for Assessing Student Learning

Teachers establish and clearly communicate learning goals for all students. Teachers collect information about student performance from a variety of sources. Teachers involve all students in assessing their own learning. Teachers use information from a variety of ongoing assessments to plan and adjust learning opportunities that promote academic achievement and personal growth for all students. Teachers exchange information about student learning with students, families, and support personnel in ways that improve understanding and encourage further academic progress.

Establishing and communicating learning goals for all students.

As teachers develop, they may ask, "How do I . . ." or "Why do I . . ."

- use subject matter standards from district, state, and other sources to guide how I establish learning goals for each student?
- involve all students and families in establishing goals for learning?
- review and revise learning goals with every student over time?
- ensure that student learning goals reflect the key subject matter concepts, skills, and applications?
- ensure that goals for learning are appropriate to my students' development, language acquisition, or other special needs?
- ensure that my grading system reflects goals for student learning?
- work with other educators to establish learning goals and assessment tools that promote student learning?

Collecting and using multiple sources of information to assess student learning.

As teachers develop, they may ask, "How do I . . ." Or "Why do I . . ."

- use a variety of assessments to determine what students know and are able to do?
- select, design, and use assessment tools appropriate to what is being assessed?
- know that the assessment tools I use are matched to and support my goals for student learning?
- collect, select, and reflect upon evidence of student learning?
- work with families to gather information about all students and their learning?
- ensure that my grades are based on multiple sources of information?
- assess my students to support student learning goals, district standards, and family expectations?
- use standardized tests, diagnostic tools, and developmental assessments to understand student progress?
- use a range of assessment strategies to implement and monitor individualized student learning goals (including IEP goals)?

Involving and guiding all students in assessing their own learning.

As teachers develop, they may ask, "How do I . . ." or "Why do I . . ."

- make assessment integral to the learning process?
- model assessment strategies for all students?
- develop and use tools and guidelines that help all students assess their own work?
- help all students to build their skills in self-reflection?
- provide opportunities for all students to engage in peer discussion of their work?
- help all students to understand and monitor their own learning goals?
- provide opportunities for all students to demonstrate and reflect on their learning inside and outside of the classroom?

Using the results of assessments to guide instruction.

As teachers develop, they may ask, "How do I . . ." Or "Why do I . . ."

- use assessment to guide my planning?
- use informal assessments of student learning to adjust instruction while teaching?
- use assessment data to plan more effective ways of teaching subject matter concepts and processes?
- use assessment information to determine when and how to revisit content that has been taught?
- use assessment data to meet students' individual needs?
- use assessment results to plan instruction to support students' individual education plans (IEP)?

Communicating with students, families, and other audiences about student progress.

As teachers develop, they may ask, "How do I . . ." or "Why do I . . ."

- provide all students with information about their progress as they engage in learning activities?
- provide opportunities for all students to share their progress with others?
- communicate learning goals to all students and their families?
- initiate and maintain regular contact with families and resource providers about student progress?
- communicate the results of assessments with my students and their families?
- involve families as partners in the assessment process?

Appendix B-3: Continuum for Assessing Student Learning

Note to the reader: This excerpt from *A Developmental Continuum of Teacher Abilities* is linked to the last element of the California Standards (Appendix B-2)

Element:	Beginning	Emerging	Applying	Integrating	In...
Communicating with students, families, and other audiences about student progress	Teacher provides students with information about their progress through test scores, grades, and report cards.	Provides students with information about their current progress as they engage in learning activities and at regularly scheduled reporting periods.	Provides students with information about their current progress and helps students use the information to improve achievement.	Provides all students with information about their progress over time and helps students use the data to improve their achievement.	Uses a assessm provide with comprehensive information about their progress over time. Helps all students to engage in reflection about their growth over time.
	Teacher communicates with families at regularly scheduled times.	Initiates communication with families and support personnel at regularly scheduled times and when needed.	Maintains regular communication with all families and support personnel to exchange information about students' social and academic progress.	Exchanges information with all families and support personnel to improve understanding and encourage social and academic progress. Students have opportunities to participate.	Involves families and support personnel as partners in the assessment process to improve understanding and encourage social and academic progress. Students share their progress and may lead conferences.

Developed by Ellen Moir, University of California at Santa Cruz, Susan Freeman, Lynne Petrock, and Wendy Baron.
Reprinted by permission of the publisher from *A Developmental Continuum of Teacher Abilities*, © 1998 Santa Cruz New Teacher Project/New Teacher Center.

References

Allen, D. (1998). The tuning protocol: Opening up reflection. In D. Allen (Ed.), *Assessing student learning: From grading to understanding* (pp. 87–104). New York: Teachers College Press.

Allen, L., Rogers, D., Hensley, F., Glanton, M., & Livingston, M. (1999). *A guide to renewing your school: Lessons from the League of Professional Schools*. San Francisco: Jossey-Bass.

Annenberg Institute for School Reform. (1999). *Looking at student work: A window into the classroom* [Videotape]. New York: Teachers College Press.

Ayers, W. (1993). *To teach: The journey of a teacher*. New York: Teachers College Press.

Blythe, T., Allen, D., & Powell, B. S. (1999). *Looking together at student work: A companion guide to assessing student learning*. New York: Teachers College Press.

Calhoun, E. F. (1994). *How to use action research in the self-renewing school*. Alexandria, VA: Association for Supervision and Curriculum Development.

California Commission on Teaching Credentialing (1997, July). *California standards for the teaching profession*. Sacramento: California Department of Education.

Cogan, M. (1973). *Clinical supervision*. Boston: Houghton Mifflin.

Costa, A., & Garmston, R. J. (1994). *Cognitive coaching: A foundation for renaissance schools*. Norwood, MA: Christopher-Gordon Publishers.

Danielson, C. (1996). *Enhancing professional practice: A framework for teaching*. Alexandria, VA: Association for Supervision and Curriculum Development.

Dayton, J. (2000, May 23). Personal communication.

Delpit, L. (1994). *Other people's children: Cultural conflict in the classroom*. New York: New Press.

DiPardo, A. (1999). *Teaching in common: Challenges to joint work in classrooms and schools*. New York: Teachers College Press.

Edmonds, R. (1979). Effective schools for the urban poor. *Educational Leadership 37*(1): 15-24.

Educational Testing Service. (1999a). *Introduction to a framework for teaching: Leader notes*. Princeton, NJ: Author.

Educational Testing Service. (1999b). *Introduction to a framework for teaching: Participant guide*. Princeton, NJ: Author.

Glickman, C. D. (1980). *Developmental supervision: Alternative practices for helping teachers to improve instruction*. Alexandria, VA: Association for Supervision and Curriculum Development.

Glickman, C. D. (1987). *Instructional improvement and the K–8 principal*. NAESP Streamlined Seminar 5(4).

Glickman, C. D. (1993). *Renewing America's schools: A guide for school-based action*. San Francisco: Jossey-Bass.

Glickman, C. D. (1998). *Revolutionizing America's schools*. San Francisco: Jossey-Bass.

Glickman, C. D., Gordon, S. P., & Ross-Gordon, J. M. (2001). *SuperVision and instructional leadership: A developmental approach* (5th ed.). Boston: Allyn and Bacon.

Goldhammer, R. (1969). *Clinical supervision: Special methods for the supervision of teachers*. New York: Holt, Rinehart, & Winston, Inc.

Good, T. L., & Brophy, J. E. (2000). *Looking in classrooms* (8th ed.). New York: Longman.

Gordon, S. P. (1991). *How to help beginning teachers succeed*. Alexandria, VA: Association for Supervision and Curriculum Development.

Lieberman, A., & Miller, L. (2001). *Teachers caught in the action: Professional development that matters*. New York: Teachers College Press.

McDonald, J. P. (1992). *Teaching: Making sense of an uncertain craft*. New York: Teachers College Press.

McDonald, J. P. (1996). *Redesigning school: Lessons for the 21st century*. San Francisco: Jossey-Bass.

McDonald, J. P. (2001). Students' work and teachers' learning. In Lieberman, A., & Miller, L. (Eds). *Teachers caught in the action: Professional development that works*. New York: Teachers College Press.

Meier, D. (1995). *The power of their ideas: Lessons for America from a small school in Harlem*. Boston: Beacon Press.

National Commission on Teaching and America's Future. (1996). *What matters most: Teaching for America's future*. New York: Author.

Nave, B. (2000). Critical friends groups: Their impact on students, teachers, and schools. [Unpublished report]. Providence, RI: Annenberg Institute for School Reform, Brown University.

Pajak, F. (2000). *Approaches to clinical supervision: Alternatives for improving instruction* (2nd ed.). Norwood, MA: Christopher-Gordon.

Palmer, P. J. (1998). *The courage to teach: Exploring the inner landscape of a teacher's life*. San Francisco: Jossey-Bass.

Rallis, F. S., & MacMullen, M. M. (2000). Inquiry-minded schools: Opening doors for accountability. *Phi Delta Kappan, 81*(10), 766–773.

Robinson, T. L., & Howard-Hamilton, M. F. (2000). *The convergence of race, identity, and gender: Multiple identities in counseling*. Columbus, OH: Merrill.

Rural Challenge Research and Evaluation Program. (1999). *Living and learning in rural schools and communities: Lessons from the field. A report to the Annenberg Rural Challenge*. Cambridge, MA: Harvard Graduate School of Education.

Santa Cruz New Teacher Project/New Teacher Center. (1998). *A developmental continuum of teacher abilities*. Santa Cruz, CA: Santa Cruz New Teacher Center.

Schmoker, M. (1999). *Results: The key to continuous school improvement* (2nd ed.). Alexandria, VA: Association for Supervision and Curriculum Development.

Sizer, T. (1992). *Horace's compromise: The dilemma of the American high school*. Boston: Houghton Mifflin.

Spalding, E. (2000). Performance assessments and the new standards project: A store of serendipitous success. *Phi Delta Kappan, 81*(10), 758–764.

Weis, C. (2000). Measuring up: The API as a planning tool. *Thrust for Leadership, 29*(4) 20–24.

Wood, G. (1998). *A time to learn*. New York: Dutton.

Young, M. D., & Laible, J. (2000, September). White racism, antiracism, and school leadership preparation. *Journal of School Leadership, 10*, 374–415.

Resources

Looking at Student Work

Books

Blythe, T., Allen, D., & Powell, B. S. (1999). *Looking together at student work: A companion guide to assessing student learning.* New York: Teachers College Press. A short, readable book that describes ways for groups of faculty to examine student work together. Includes formats of "Fine Tuning Protocols" and the "Collaborative Assessment Conference." Used by thousands of K–12 schools that are members of various school renewal networks.

Glickman, C. D., Gordon, S. P., & Ross-Gordon, J. V. (2001). Observing skills. In *SuperVision and instructional leadership: A developmental approach* (5th ed.) (pp. 250–275). Boston: Allyn and Bacon. A comprehensive text on instructional leadership and supervision. This chapter describes various quantitative and qualitative observation forms and methods and how to choose one based on a particular classroom learning objective.

McDonald, J. P. (2001). Students' work and teachers' learning. In Lieberman, A., & Miller, L. (Eds). *Teachers caught in the action: The work of professional development.* New York: Teachers College Press.

A succinct chapter that explains the various traditions and methods for observing teaching and learning in classrooms and schools. Gives examples of how school faculties have used, revised, or created protocols for productive conversations and actions.

Schmoker, M. (1999). *Results: The key to continuous school improvement* (2nd ed.). Alexandria, VA: Association for Supervision and Curriculum Development. One of the most widely used books by school leaders in the United States. The author describes ways for schools to collect and analyze student achievement data to determine learning goals and actions. This short book is full of examples, cases, and guidelines.

Video

Annenberg Institute for School Reform. (1997). *Looking at student work: A window into the classroom.* New York: Teachers College Press. A 28-minute video that is of great help in preparing school leaders and faculty to use group formats for looking together at student work. The video contains actual footage of teachers and administrators in such meetings and is a nice staff development companion to the book by Blythe, Allen, and Powell (1999) mentioned earlier.

Web sites

http://www.l asw.org

The interactive Web site *Looking at Student Work* seeks to inform educators and school community partners about the benefits and challenges of looking collaboratively at student work and teacher practice at all levels. The site was developed by more than two dozen individuals and organizations—among them, the Education Trust, Harvard Project Zero, Chicago Learning Collaborative, the

League of Professional Schools, the Southern Maine Partnership, and the Coalition of Essential Schools. The Annenberg Institute for School Reform hosts the site in conjunction with the National School Reform Faculty. The Web site offers the following:

- Rationale: Purposes and principles for examining student work
- Examples: Student work samples and session transcripts
- Resources: Methods and protocols for looking at student work
- Guidelines: First steps, cautions, and tips for getting started
- Dialogue: Questions, lessons learned, success stories
- Contacts: People and organizations interested in this work

http://www.newteachercenter.org

The New Teacher Center of the University of California–Santa Cruz explores good teaching, effective evaluation, and observation and coaching conferences. Their recommendations are based on more than a decade of learnings that enhance teacher development.

Cultural, Ethnic, and Personal Identity

Books

Nieto, S. (1999). *The light in their eyes: Creating multicultural learning communities*. New York: Teachers College Press. In this book, Sonia Nieto clearly makes known to the reader a thorough understanding of what it takes to teach in multicultural contexts. She demonstrates her ability as a leading theorist in the field of multicultural education and critical pedagogy in this text, which is presented with wonderful clarity and expertise.

Nieto, S. (2000). *Affirming diversity: The sociopolitical context of multicultural education*. New York: Longman. This is an excellent textbook for anyone involved in the field of education. It reads fairly easily and uses case studies to give insight to lessons. The case studies bring light to the experience of being a member of a minority group. The book is written with sensitivity and intelligence. Sonia Nieto is not afraid to write about the struggle, frustration, and pain that minorities experience.

Paley, V. (2000). *White teacher*. Cambridge, MA: Harvard University Press. Vivian Paley presents a moving personal account of her experiences teaching kindergarten in an integrated school within a predominantly white, middle-class neighborhood. In a new preface, she reflects on the way that even simple terminology can convey unintended meanings and show a speaker's blind spots. She also vividly describes what her readers have taught her over the years about herself as a "white teacher."

Articles

Guess, G. (1997, October). Breaking down barriers: Menlo-Atherton High School. *Thrust for Educational Leadership, 27,* 16–18. Menlo-Atherton High School in California created a cultural diversity–training program for its freshman class to help students become more aware of the different cultures at the school. The aim was to provide students with an early introduction to high school, foster camaraderie with their peers, and help younger students identify with the junior and senior students who would serve as their peer facilitators. The program was developed with the help of parents, and students were involved in planning programs that would focus on the strengths of diversity.

McKee, A., & Schor, S. M. (1999). Confronting prejudice and stereotypes: A teaching model. *Performance Improvement Quarterly, 12*(1), 181–199. As the demographics of the workforce continue to change dramatically and the globalization of the marketplace escalates, it becomes increasingly important for employees, managers, and leaders to value differences and to work effectively with people of various cultures, backgrounds, races, genders, sexual orientations, and language groups. The competencies and skills necessary for effectively working across these boundaries do not necessarily come naturally, and it is increasingly essential for organizations to provide opportunities for people to develop the capacity to deal with volatile issues such as diversity, prejudice, and stereotyping.

Panitz, B. (1996, April). Lessons in diversity: Three approaches to making faculty aware of multicultural issues. *ASEE Prism, 5,* 14–15. The writer discusses three different approaches to diversity training and making faculty members aware of multicultural issues. The DuPont Multicultural Awareness Workshop, a corporate model, is a diversity training program offered to DuPont employees that is also available, free of charge, to a limited number of engineering educators. The National Action Council for Minorities in Engineering's diversity seminars are based on the corporate model but are tailored to the specific needs of engineering schools. The Faculty Advisors for Minority Engineering Students (FAMES) program focused on two main areas: training in developmental counseling and training in cultural awareness and cross-cultural communication. Although FAMES is no longer running, it is used as a model for other diversity training efforts.

Rodriguez, D. M. (1998, September). Diversity training brings staff closer. *Education Digest, 64*(1), 28–31. This is a condensed version of an article from the January edition of the *American School Board Journal.* The aim of diversity training is to create a forum for people to question and critique their beliefs. Diversity days involve frank discussion between school district employees on subjects such as race, gender, sexual orientation, disabilities, and individual differences.

Wilson, J. B. (1998, Spring/Summer). Diversity training with a dramatic flair. *CUPA Journal, 49*(1–2), 27–30. A diversity training initiative at the University of Wisconsin–La Crosse involves social action theater. Participants in the United We Learn Social Action Theatre present brief plays developed on the basis of their experiences or of campus or community events. A diversity issue is presented in the play in a way that creates a conflict among the actors. When the conflict reaches a critical juncture, a moderator halts the action and calls on audience members to ask the actors questions. After the first question-and-answer period, the moderator again stops the action. Eventually, the actors introduce themselves and answer questions from the audience on the basis of their real-life experiences.

Videos

Blue Eyed. Produced by Claus Strigel and Bertram Verhagg. *Blue Eyed* offers diversity trainers and human resource managers their first chance to sit in on a full-length video workshop with diversity trainer Jane Elliott. Elliott contends, "A person who has been raised and socialized in America has been conditioned to be a racist. We live in two countries, one black and one white." In contrast to the usual encounter-group strategy, Elliott believes it's important for whites to experience the emotional impact of discrimination for themselves. In *Blue Eyed,* viewers join a diverse group of 40 employees from the Midwest—blacks, Hispanics, whites, women, and men. The blue-eyed members participate in an exercise that involves a pseudo-scientific explanation of their inferiority, culturally biased IQ tests, and blatant disrespect.

It's Elementary: Talking About Gay Issues in School. Produced by
Women's Educational Media. With inspiring footage shot in
schools across the country, *It's Elementary* shows real examples of
school activities, faculty meetings, and classroom discussions about
lesbian and gay issues. This beautifully crafted video and the accompanying viewing guide are designed to open constructive dialogue
among the adults in school communities about one of the most con-
troversial issues facing schools today.

Teaching Respect for All. Produced by GLSEN (Gay, Lesbian, and
Straight Education Network). A stunning 97 percent of high school
students report regularly hearing epithets such as "faggot" and
"dyke" in their schools. Yet many schools think that prejudice
against gay and lesbian people is not their problem or is something
"inappropriate" to address in the school setting. In this educational
training video, GLSEN executive director and former high school
teacher Kevin Jennings helps a live audience of parents, teachers,
administrators, and other concerned citizens to understand why
schools must address anti-gay prejudice if all students are to achieve
their educational potential.

Web Sites

http://www.hrpress-diversity.com/booklst.html
Books and videos produced by HR Press dealing with diversity.

http://www.diversityuintl.com/resource.htm
Web site for Diversity Training University International. Provides
information on how to do diversity training as well as links to
resources and bibliographies of books and articles. Geared more
toward general diversity training—not specifically schools, but
could be easily adapted to an educational setting.

http://www.rctm.com/

Website for The Richardson Company Training Media. Not specifically geared to education, but adaptable because it deals with diversity in the workplace. Includes some excellent diversity training programs on video.

http://www.glsen.org

Website for the Gay, Lesbian, and Straight Education Network. Provides information about gays and lesbians in schools as well as links to resources and information.

http://www.splcenter.org/teachingtolerance/tt-index.html

General Web site for Teaching Tolerance. Includes information about *Teaching Tolerance Magazine* as well as resources for teachers about teaching respect for diversity. Includes links to information about grants and teaching materials.

http://www.naacp.org
http://www.academicinfo.net/africanam.html
African American issues.

http://www.getnet.net/~1stbooks/
Hispanic issues.

http://www.umich.edu/~uaao/
Asian American issues.

http://nativeweb.org
Native American issues.

http://www.hrpress-diversity.com/videolst.html
Videos produced by HR Press dealing with diversity.

Structures and Formats for Professional Development and Instructional Leadership

From Educational Testing Service

Comprehensive Programs for Professional Development
Pathwise Leadership Academy.
Web site: www.teachingandlearning.org/
E-mail: pathwise@mktgworks.com.

More From ASCD

Arredondo, D., Zimmerman, D., & Brody, J. *Transforming supervision: A framework for collaborative leadership* [Audiotape]. Explains a model of collaborative leadership that provides specific knowledge and skills for promoting collaborative professional relationships and transforms supervision through reculturing, reflective practice, and dialogue about learning (stock no. 297083S25).

Calhoun, E. (1994). *How to use action research in the self-renewing school.* The author shows how to use action research in change efforts to ensure that such efforts positively influence student learning and contribute to a more positive learning climate (stock no. 194030; ISBN 0-87120-229-8).

Danielson, C. (1996). *Enhancing professional practice: A framework for teaching.* This 140-page softcover book includes a complete description of the 22 components of professional practice within the four major domains of teaching. This framework (see Appendix B-1 in this book) is an extension of the author's earlier work with the Educational Testing Service on PRAXIS III: Classroom Performance

Assessments. Grounded in research, the original PRAXIS III has here been augmented to apply to experienced, as well as to novice, teachers. Rubrics are included to identify levels of performance for each domain. Chapter 5 discusses uses of the framework for reflection and self-assessment, for mentoring and induction, for peer coaching, and for supervision, making the book useful in implementing the various approaches in this book (stock no. 196074; ISBN 0-87120-269-7).

Danielson, C., & McGreal, T. (2000). *Teacher evaluation to enhance professional practice*. This recent publication places the use of the Framework for Teaching (see Appendix B-1 in this book) as a central feature in teacher evaluation and categorizes those evaluation processes as Track I for beginning teachers, Track II for tenured teachers, and Track III for tenured teachers needing assistance. The authors present concrete examples, useful forms, and assessment tools. Published jointly with Educational Testing Service (stock no. 100219; ISBN 0-87120-380-4).

DuFour, R., & Eaker, R. (1998). *Professional learning communities at work: Best practices for enhancing student achievement*. This book shows educators how to sustain school improvement by helping staff function as a professional learning community in which teachers are committed to ongoing study, constant practice, and mutual cooperation. Presents the essential building blocks of effective schools and ways to sustain change efforts through better communication and collaboration (stock no. 198188; ISBN 1-879639-60-2).

Glickman, C. (Ed.). (1992). *Supervision in transition* (1992 ASCD yearbook). This 222-page yearbook presents the most recent definitive overview of issues and developments in the area of supervision. The yearbook is organized in four major sections: (1) The Context, featuring policy relationships, purposes, and changing perspectives; (2)

The Practice, describing concrete examples from school districts; (3) The Preparation, focusing on collegial support, student teaching experiences, and professional inquiry processes; and (4) The Reflection, offering views on the transformation and regeneration of supervision. A variety of authors, from well-established university scholars to highly respected district practitioners, contributed the individual chapters. Provides excellent understanding of the development of supervision over time and explores the various influences on the practice of supervision (stock no. 61092000; ISBN 0-87120-188-7).

Glickman, C. (1995). *On action research* [Audiotape]. This 60-minute tape offers many examples of common issues that can be addressed by action research. The uses of action research are extended to applications with students. The tape explains how the process of involving students in problem solving and policymaking helps to build a democratic school environment (stock no. 295190).

Glickman, C., & Calhoun, E. (1995). *Action research: Inquiry, reflection, and decision making* [Video series]. This package includes a series of four videotapes demonstrating the use of action research in identifying and solving problems in classrooms and organizations, plus a 289-page Facilitator's Guide and a copy of *How to Use Action Research in the Self-Renewing School*. The first video is an overview that describes the five phases of the action research cycle; the other three videos are case studies that show how action research has guided improvement efforts at an elementary school, a high school, and throughout an entire district (stock no. 495037).

Miles, E. (2000). *Peer coaching: Establishing a community of learners* [Audiotape]. From the 2000 ASCD Annual Conference. Focuses on how peer coaching helps teachers with continued growth and development. Provides implementation suggestions for any school setting. Explains what works and what doesn't, along with reactions from teachers who have participated in peer coaching (stock no. 200074).

Rowley, J. M., & Hart, P. M. (1994). *Mentoring the new teacher* [Video series]. These eight videos include the following titles: (1) Dealing with Students' Personal Problems, (2) Classroom Discipline, (3) Dealing with Individual Differences, (4) Motivating Students, (5) Planning Classwork, (6) Lack of Instructional Resources, (7) Parent Relations, and (8) Evaluating Student Work. Developed and produced by Rowley and Hart at the University of Dayton, Dayton, Ohio, in 1994; available exclusively through ASCD (stock no. 494002).

Scherer, M. (Ed.). (1999). *A better beginning: Supporting and mentoring new teachers.* This 240-page compilation features case studies of successful programs combined with the practical experiences of seasoned administrators and teacher leaders. Presents various options for induction programs and emphasizes mentoring programs that benefit all teachers involved. Also relates to systemwide programs of induction and mentoring programs with ongoing assessment and professional development (stock no. 199236; ISBN 0-87120-355-3).

Wald, P. J., & Castleberry, M. S. (2000). *Educators as learners: Creating a professional learning community in your school.* This 128-page guide offers practical, field-tested insights and approaches to developing teamwork, commitment, and shared responsibility for student success. Presents leadership qualities essential to collaboration, along with the key stages of the collaborative learning process and group practices that support collaborative learning. Features planning tools for the development of ongoing staff development programs (stock no. 100005; ISBN 0-87120-366-9).

Another set of eyes [Video]. (1989). This series of videos shows extensive footage of conferencing techniques for clinical supervision and peer coaching, followed by superb visuals and descriptions of the communication techniques that contribute to success in the use of these processes (stock no. 614179).

Opening doors [Video]. (1989). This package introduces the concept of peer coaching with ample illustration of the pre-conference, the observation, and the postconference. Presents excellent examples of collegial relationships maintained during the clinical supervision sequence (stock no. 614182).

For additional resources, visit ASCD on the World Wide Web (www.ascd.org), send an e-mail message to member@ascd.org, call the ASCD Service Center (1-800-933-2723 or 703-575-9600), send a fax to 703-575-5400, or write to Information Services, ASCD, 1703 N. Beauregard St., Alexandria, VA 22311-1714 USA.

Index

About the Author

Carl D. Glickman is President of the Institute for Schools, Education, and Democracy in Athens, Georgia, Chair of the Program for School Improvement, and University Professor Emeritus of Education at the University of Georgia. He received his bachelor's degree from Colby College in Maine, his master's degree from Hampton University in Virginia, and his doctoral degree from the University of Virginia. He has been a principal of award-winning schools, the author of a leading academic text on school leadership, and a three-time recipient of the outstanding teacher award in the College of Education at the University of Georgia. In 1997 he was awarded the highest faculty career honor of the University of Georgia for bringing "stature and distinction" to the mission of the university. Students recognized him in 1999 as the faculty member who has contributed most to their lives, inside and outside of the classroom.

For the past 20 years, he has founded and headed various university/public school collaborations, including the nationally renowned League of Professional Schools. These initiatives involved more than one hundred elementary, middle, and secondary schools representing 50 school districts in four states focused on school renewal through democratic education. These efforts were recognized as among the most outstanding educational collaborations in the United States by the National Business–Higher Education Forum, the U.S. Department of Education, and the Merrow Group of the U.S. Public Broadcasting System.

Dr. Glickman has authored 12 books and numerous articles, studies, and essays. His books *Renewing America's Schools* (Jossey-Bass), *Revolutionizing America's Schools* (Jossey-Bass), and *SuperVision and Instructional Leadership* with Stephen P. Gordon and Jovita M. Ross-Gordon (Allyn and Bacon) have been cited as standards for all those committed to the public purpose of education. He and his wife, Sara, reside in Athens, Georgia, and St. Albans Bay, Vermont. He can be contacted at the Institute for Schools, Education, and Democracy (ISEDINC@aol.com).